OCCASIONAL
P A P E R

Reducing Drug Trafficking Revenues and Violence in Mexico

Would Legalizing Marijuana in California Help?

Beau Kilmer, Jonathan P. Caulkins,
Brittany M. Bond, Peter H. Reuter

RAND INTERNATIONAL PROGRAMS and
DRUG POLICY RESEARCH CENTER

Funding for this study was provided by RAND International Programs through RAND's Investment in People and Ideas program, which combines philanthropic contributions from individuals, foundations, and private-sector firms with earnings from RAND's endowment and operations to support research on issues that reach beyond the scope of traditional client sponsorship.

Library of Congress Control Number: 2010938755

ISBN: 978-0-8330-5107-3

Published 2010 by the RAND Corporation
1776 Main Street, P.O. Box 2138, Santa Monica, CA 90407-2138
1200 South Hayes Street, Arlington, VA 22202-5050
4570 Fifth Avenue, Suite 600, Pittsburgh, PA 15213-2665
RAND URL: http://www.rand.org/
To order RAND documents or to obtain additional information, contact
Distribution Services: Telephone: (310) 451-7002;
Fax: (310) 451-6915; Email: order@rand.org

Preface

U.S. demand for illicit drugs creates markets for Mexican drug trafficking organizations (DTOs). This paper examines how marijuana legalization in California might influence DTO revenues and the violence in Mexico, focusing on gross revenues from export and distribution to wholesale markets near the southwestern U.S. border. The analysis described here is rooted in an earlier RAND Corporation study on marijuana legalization (Kilmer, Caulkins, Pacula, et al., 2010) and presents a method of estimating the revenues that international drug traffickers derive from U.S. sales that is transparent and, hence, auditable and replicable. We believe that this method can be iteratively improved by research over time, whereas existing methods that rely heavily on classified information have not been subject to review and have not shown much ongoing improvement.

Five technical appendixes include additional information about the weight of a marijuana joint, THC content of sinsemilla and commercial-grade marijuana, marijuana prices, Mexican DTO revenues from drugs other than marijuana, and the availability of Mexican marijuana in the U.S. They are available online at http://www.rand.org/pubs/occasional_papers/OP325/.

This research was conducted under the auspices of RAND International Programs with funding from RAND's Investment in People and Ideas program, which combines philanthropic contributions from individuals, foundations, and private-sector firms with earnings from RAND's endowment and operations to support research on issues that reach beyond the scope of traditional client sponsorship. RAND International Programs facilitates research on regionally and internationally focused topics for a wide range of U.S. as well as international clients, including governments, foundations, and corporations. For more information on RAND International Programs, see http://www.rand.org/international_programs/about/ or contact the director (contact information is provided on the web page).

Contents

Figures

Tables

Acknowledgments

We would like to thank Martin Bouchard, Mark Kleiman, Greg Ridgeway, K. Jack Riley, and Paul Steinberg for their comments and recommendations. We are especially indebted to Susan Everingham, Rosalie Liccardo Pacula, Eric Sevigny, and David Shirk for their detailed and extremely useful reviews. We would also like to thank Eric Sevigny for providing prisoner survey data and Greg Ridgeway for statistical assistance. As always, Jim Burgdorf provided excellent research assistance. The views presented here are solely those of the authors.

Abbreviations

ADAM	Arrestee Drug Abuse Monitoring (program)
DEA	Drug Enforcement Administration
DFS	Dirección Federal de Seguridad
DTO	drug-trafficking organization
FARC	Fuerzas Armadas Revolucionarias de Colombia
FBI	Federal Bureau of Investigation
g	gram
GAO	U.S. Government Accountability Office
IDPPR	*Illegal Drug Price/Purity Report*
INCSR	*International Narcotics Control Strategy Report*
kg	kilogram
LSD	lysergic acid diethylamide
mg	milligram
MT	metric ton
MTF	Monitoring the Future
NDCS	*National Drug Control Strategy*
NDIC	National Drug Intelligence Center
NHSDA	*National Household Survey on Drug Abuse*
NSDUH	*National Survey on Drug Use and Health*
PAN	Partido Acción Nacional
PRI	Partido Revolucionario Institucional
SAMHSA	Substance Abuse and Mental Health Services Administration
STRATFOR	Strategic Forecasting

TEDS	*Treatment Episode Data Set*
THC	tetrahydrocannabinol
UN	United Nations
UNODC	United Nations Office on Drugs and Crime
WDR	*World Drug Report*

CHAPTER ONE

Introduction

The recent surge in violence in Mexico has been dramatic. While the per capita murder rate fell by roughly 25 percent between 2000 and 2007, it jumped 50 percent between 2007 and 2009 (Sistema Nacional de Seguridad Pública and Consejo Nacional de Población, 2010). The violence associated with the illicit drug trade is largely responsible for this reversal. The estimated annual total for drug-related homicides in Mexico increased from 1,776 in 2005 to 6,587 in 2009, and, in 2010, the total was already 5,775 by July (Duran-Martinez, Hazard, and Rios, 2010; Shirk, 2010). In 2009, the murder rate for drug-related homicides alone in Mexico exceeded the rate for all murders and nonnegligent manslaughters in the United States (6.1 versus 5.1 per 100,000; Shirk, 2010; FBI, 2010).

This violence in Mexico has security implications for the United States. The primary problem to date has *not* been violence spilling over the border. While there have been such incidents, and some are quite horrific, homicide rates in the U.S. cities along the Mexican border remain very low. El Paso is the second-safest city in the United States, with just 2.8 homicides per 100,000 (Borunda, 2009)—a rate that is lower than that of Paris or Geneva. This is in sharp contrast to El Paso's twin city in Mexico, Ciudad Juárez, which experienced 2,754 homicides in 2009 (a rate of 196.7 per 100,000). While spillover violence does have important security implications for those living and working north of the border, this threat might have been exaggerated and pales in comparison to the lawlessness that pervades parts of Mexico. The bigger security implication for the United States is having a close ally and a large trading partner engulfed in such turmoil.[1]

Demand for illicit drugs in the United States creates lucrative markets for the Mexican drug-trafficking organizations (DTOs). Secretary of State Hillary Clinton, echoing President George W. Bush in 2001, noted that America's demand for drugs was a root cause of the violence. While this has led some to argue that priority should be given to reducing U.S. drug demand, Reuter's (2010, p. 3) assessment of the literature leads him to soberly conclude that "there is little that the U.S. can do to reduce consumption over the next five years that will help Mexico." This does not mean that a serious investment in reducing consumption among heavy users (especially those in criminal justice settings) is not good policy (see Kleiman, 2009). It just means that one should not expect rapid results. The great bulk of drug demand comes from the minority of individuals who are the heavy users (Everingham, Rydell, and Caulkins, 1995; Rhodes et al., 1997; Kilmer and Pacula, 2009); reducing their consumption is difficult.

---

[1] Approximately 10 percent of Mexico's federal police force was dismissed on August 30, 2010, for failing "basic competence tests" (Thomson, 2010).

Legalizing drugs has been suggested as a quicker and more decisive solution to the violence. Most notably, former Mexican president Vicente Fox recently called for Mexico to legalize the production, distribution, and sale of all drugs as a way of reducing the DTOs' power and related violence. He advocated it "as a strategy to weaken and break the economic system that allows cartels to earn huge profits" (Rosenberg, 2010). Mexico's current president, Felipe Calderón, does not support legalization, but he has said that legalization should be a topic of discussion ("Thinking the Unthinkable," 2010).

The consequences of Mexico unilaterally legalizing drug production and distribution are fairly easy to foresee. Legalization would limit DTO revenues from drug distribution in Mexico to revenues only derived from evading any associated taxes and regulations. However, unless the United States followed suit, Mexican DTOs would continue to profit by illegally smuggling drugs across the border. Comprehensive data on DTO's full portfolio of revenues are understandably scarce, but no one believes that distribution to Mexican users is the primary revenue generator for DTOs.

Not surprisingly, violence in Mexico plays a prominent role in debates about marijuana legalization in the United States. Often, big numbers of dubious origin are tossed around in drug policy discussions with little thought and, frankly, little consequence. Some U.S. government reports suggest that Mexican and Colombian DTOs combined earn $18 billion–$39 billion annually in wholesale drug proceeds (NDIC, 2008d), and one analysis even estimated that 60 percent of all Mexican DTO drug revenue comes from exporting marijuana (ONDCP, 2006). Legalization advocates seize on such figures to supplement their traditional arguments, and the figures have been repeated in the popular press, with even respectable news sources claiming that "the Mexican cartels could be selling $20 billion worth of marijuana in the U.S. market each year" (Fainaru and Booth, 2009).

The $20 billion figure appears to come from multiplying a $525-per-pound[2] markup by an estimate from the Mexican government that 35 million pounds were produced in Mexico and then rounding up. However, no data support the claim that U.S. users consume 35 million pounds (~16,000 metric tons [MT]) per year, let alone that they consume this much marijuana from Mexico. (This point is addressed in detail in Chapter Three.) This is *three* times the United Nations Office on Drugs and Crime's (UNODC) (2009) upper bound for total U.S. consumption and nearly *four* times the amount estimated by the Drug Enforcement Administration (DEA) (DASC, 2002).

Nevertheless, the wide acceptance of such large numbers may have substantial consequences. In November 2010, California voters will decide on Proposition 19 (also known as the Regulate, Control and Tax Cannabis Act of 2010, or Prop 19). Proposition 19 would legalize marijuana possession for those 21 and older, permit adults to cultivate 5-foot-by-5-foot plots in their homes, and allow each local jurisdiction to enable, regulate, and tax commercial production and distribution. Advocates have argued that legalizing marijuana in California will reduce the role the Mexican DTOs play in supplying marijuana, thereby reducing violence. In particular, the official ballot argument for Proposition 19[3] states that "[m]arijuana prohibition has created vicious drug cartels across our border," and a proponent's website claims that Prop-

---

[2]   One pound equals 0.45359237 kg.

[3]   For each ballot proposition, official statements of the arguments for and against the proposition are distributed to voters in advance (California Secretary of State, 2010).

osition 19 will "[c]ut off funding to violent drug cartels across our border who currently generate 60 percent of their revenue from the illegal U.S. marijuana market" (Yes on 19, undated).

This paper seeks to provide a better understanding of how marijuana legalization in California could influence DTO revenues and the violence in Mexico. We focus on gross revenues from export and distribution to wholesale markets near the southwestern U.S. border. DTOs also generate revenue from operations further down the distribution chain in the United States. It is difficult to assess how much they make from such domestic (U.S.) distribution, and it is unclear how this would change postlegalization because distribution would become legal only for one drug in one state. The analysis is rooted in RAND's earlier report on marijuana legalization (Kilmer, Caulkins, Pacula, et al., 2010) and provides a number of important, albeit preliminary, insights about the markets for cocaine, heroin, and methamphetamine.

In this paper we also put forward a transparent, and hence, auditable and replicable, method of estimating the revenues that international drug traffickers derive from U.S. sales. We believe that the method we use and discuss in this paper can be iteratively improved by research over time, whereas existing methods that rely heavily on classified information have not been subject to review and have not shown much ongoing improvement.

Our analysis leads to the following insights:

- Mexican DTOs' gross revenues from moving marijuana across the border into the United States and selling it to wholesalers is likely less than $2 billion, and our preferred estimate is closer to $1.5 billion. This figure does not include revenue from DTO production and distribution in the United States, which is extremely difficult to estimate with existing data.

- The ubiquitous claim that 60 percent of Mexican DTO export revenues come from U.S. marijuana consumption (Fainaru and Booth, 2009; Yes on 19, undated) should not be taken seriously. No publicly available source verifies or explains this figure and subsequent analyses revealed great uncertainty about the estimate (GAO, 2007). Our analysis—though preliminary on this point—suggests that 15–26 percent is a more credible range of the share of drug export revenues attributable to marijuna.

- California accounts for about one-seventh of U.S. marijuana consumption, and domestic production is already stronger in California than elsewhere in the United States. Hence, if Prop 19 *only* affects revenues from supplying marijuana to California, DTO drug export revenue losses would be very small, on the order of 2–4 percent.

- The only way Prop 19 could importantly cut DTO drug *export* revenues is if California-produced marijuana is smuggled to other states at prices that outcompete current Mexican supplies. The extent of such smuggling will depend on a number of factors, including the actions of the federal government and other states. It is very hard to anticipate how the conflict between state, federal, and international law engendered by Prop 19 would play out, but it is important to note that hopes for substantially undermining DTO revenues are contingent on varying scenarios concerning that conflict.

- *If* marijuana can be diverted from legal production in California to other states and *if* smuggling it is no harder than it is to do today within U.S. borders, *then* California production could undercut sales of Mexican marijuana throughout much of the United States, cutting DTOs' marijuana export revenues by more than 65 percent and probably by 85 percent or more. However, there is significant uncertainty regarding the assumptions underlying this estimate, including (1) whether taxes are collected on the marijuana before it is diverted out of California's legal distribution chain, (2) how intense federal, state, and local enforcement efforts will be against that diverted marijuana, and (3) how many grams of lower-potency Mexican marijuana consumers will see as being equivalent to one gram of higher-potency, California-grown sinsemilla (i.e., how closely users view the two forms of the drug as substitutes).

- It is unclear whether reductions in Mexican DTOs' revenues from exporting marijuana would lead to corresponding decreases in violence. Some mechanisms suggest that large reductions in revenues could increase violence in the short run but decrease it in the long run.

- Drug markets are intrinsically difficult to measure, and estimates will never be precise. However, some of the current uncertainty stems from parameters that are not hard to study, such as the weight of an average marijuana joint. That the best nationally representative data on something so simple is almost 20 years old and is calculated indirectly reflects how disconnected data-collection agencies are from the policy process, and vice versa.

With respect to whether marijuana legalization in California could help reduce the violence in Mexico, our best answer is "not to any appreciable extent unless California exports drive Mexican marijuana out of the market in other states; if that happens, in the long run, possibly yes, but unlikely much in the short run." There is no quick, politically feasible fix to reducing the DTO violence in Mexico. As a number of other researchers have noted, there are fundamental issues related to the justice system that need to be addressed before anyone can expect significant improvements in the security situation in Mexico (Cornelius and Shirk, 2007; Schaefer, Bahney, and Riley, 2009; Felbab-Brown, 2009; Ingram and Shirk, 2010).

The remainder of this paper is structured as follows. Chapter Two reviews the methodologies used to estimate the size of drug markets, and Chapter Three calculates U.S. marijuana consumption and associated DTO gross export revenues. Chapter Four assesses how Mexican DTO marijuana export revenues could be affected by legalization in California. Chapter Five provides a critical assessment of the claim that 60 percent of Mexican DTO drug revenues come from marijuana and presents an exploratory analysis of DTO revenues from exporting other drugs. Chapter Six speculates how a reduction in marijuana revenues could influence Mexican DTOs and the escalating violence that surrounds them. Chapter Seven offers some concluding thoughts and ideas for advancing the research on this topic.

CHAPTER TWO

Methods for Estimating Drug-Trafficking Organizations' Drug Revenues

Our goal is to estimate how legalizing marijuana would affect the revenues earned by Mexican DTOs and how this, in turn, could affect violence in Mexico. The estimate naturally pertains to marijuana, but it is important to scale that loss of revenue relative to the DTOs' total revenues from trafficking drugs into the United States. Few people have any intuition about how useful in absolute terms it is to take $100 million or $1 billion in revenues away from the DTOs. Therefore, when it comes to projecting effects on DTO power and violence, it is easier to work from percentage reductions in their revenues, not absolute changes.

DTO revenues from transporting drugs across the Mexican–U.S. border equal the average import price times the amount delivered. There are effectively two ways of estimating this important part of DTOs' revenues. The supply-side approach multiplies the import price by production minus seizures and consumption in Mexico.[1] The demand-side approach multiplies the import price by demand-side estimates of amounts consumed in the United States after subtracting amounts supplied from sources other than Mexico (e.g., domestically produced marijuana, marijuana imported from Canada). In principle, amounts seized in the United States after the drugs are no longer in the DTOs' control should be added, because, from the DTO's perspective, these drugs generate revenue just as surely as those that reach the final user.

Hence, estimates of DTO trafficking revenues are grounded in estimates of the total size of the U.S. drug market. The focus here is on marijuana, cocaine (including crack), heroin, and methamphetamine, because they are thought to account for upwards of 95 percent of illegal drug market revenues in the United States (Abt Associates, 2001) and because Mexican DTOs do not play a prominent role in the markets for other drugs, such as ecstasy and lysergic acid diethylamide (LSD) (NDIC, 2010).

The next section reviews current strategies for estimating the size of U.S. drug markets and explains the limitations of these approaches. It focuses on the two main approaches for estimating the size of a drug market: supply-side and demand-side estimation. Following that is a section that makes a number of clarifying distinctions relevant to how our estimate of lost DTO revenues should be interpreted.

---

[1] Historically, no adjustment was made for Mexican drug use, on the grounds that it was very low. Over time, as drug use in Mexico grows (Medina-Mora et al., 2006), that simplification becomes more problematic.

Current Approaches for Estimating the Size of U.S. Drug Markets

Supply-Side Estimates

Supply-side estimates start with estimates of which we are skeptical: production estimates.[2] This skepticism stems from experience with nearly 25 years of improbable and inconsistent reporting by various government agencies and international organizations (see, e.g., Reuter, 1984, 1996). The most cited example here is the notorious difference between cocaine production estimates generated by the United Nations (UN) and those produced by the U.S. government (e.g., Reuter and Greenfield, 2001; Kilmer and Pacula, 2009; Kilmer and Reuter, 2009). The differences are likely attributable to differences in satellite imagery, assumptions about yield, and assumptions about the efficacy of eradication efforts. The largest discrepancy overall is for Colombia in 2007, with the U.S. figure being almost 70 percent larger than the estimates generated by the UN (167,000 and 99,000, respectively). The differences also fluctuate substantially over time. For example, from 1999 to 2001, the U.S. estimate increased from 122,500 to 169,800 hectares, while the UN figures decreased from 160,100 to 144,800 hectares (see Figure 2.1).

More relevant for this report is the fact that U.S. government estimates of Mexican marijuana production have long been inconsistent and sometimes implausible. Reuter (1996) highlights how various agencies in the United States not only show different levels of marijuana

Figure 2.1
UN and U.S. Estimates of Net Coca Cultivation (Hectares)

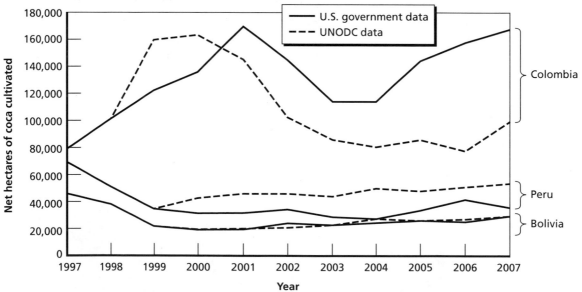

SOURCE: Kilmer and Pacula (2009, p. 68).
NOTE: UNODC uses the figures from the U.S. Department of State for the following years: Bolivia (1997–2001), Colombia (1997–1998), and Peru (1997–1999).
RAND OP325-2.1

---

[2] A related approach divides seizures by some assumed proportion of shipments that are seized, such as 10 percent. The problem with that approach is that it assumes that the share of shipments seized is constant over time, place, and drugs. In fact, there are good reasons to believe that the share seized is quite variable in each of those dimensions. For example, because marijuana is bulky compared to heroin, it might have a higher detection rate. Additionally, some U.S. entry points are better guarded than others.

production in Mexico but also exhibit opposing trends. He then addresses the "fundamental unsoundness of the whole series of estimates" with a critical discussion of the data published in the late 1980s. The 1990 *International Narcotics Control Strategy Report* (INCSR) (U.S. Department of State, 1990) shows an increase in Mexican marijuana production from 5,700 MT in 1988 to 47,000 MT in 1989 (nearly a 700-percent increase) because of "changes in estimation techniques"; however, these changes are not explained in the published document. A few years later, the 1994 INCSR presented a revised estimate for 1990, reducing the figure from 47,000 MT to a still-unbelievable 30,200 MT, which represents a more than 400-percent increase (U.S. Department of State, 1994).

There are also questions about the validity of the published marijuana production estimates for the 2000s (Table 2.1). While the supply-side estimates suggest that net production in Mexico almost tripled between 2001 and 2008, the number of current (meaning past-month) users in the United States has remained stable at 15 million. In fact, the share of high school seniors reporting daily marijuana use appears to have decreased over this period. This raises important questions about where all this marijuana is going. Marijuana seizures at the border cannot account for the discrepancy—the border seizures have hovered between 1,000 and 1,500 MT annually for most of the past decade (GAO, 2007; NDIC, 2010).

Table 2.1 also presents another example of how the same agency can provide very different numbers over time. Data from the 2009 World Drug Report (WDR) (UNODC, 2009) imply that Mexican production was almost halved between 2007 and 2008. UNODC is not

Table 2.1
Net Marijuana Production in Mexico and U.S. Marijuana Consumption

Year	Potential Net Production of Cannabis in Mexico (MT)			Past-Month U.S. Marijuana Users (millions)	Percentage of 12th Graders Reporting Daily Marijuana Use in Previous Month
	2010 INCSR	2009 WDR[a]	2010 WDR[b]	2002–2008 NSDUH[c]	2002–2008 MTF[d]
2001	7,400			e	5.8
2002	7,900			14.6	6.0
2003	13,500			14.6	6.0
2004	10,440			14.6	5.6
2005	10,100			14.6	5.0
2006	15,500			14.8	5.0
2007	15,800	27,806		14.5	5.1
2008	21,500	15,800	21,500	15.2f	5.4

NOTE: WDR = *World Drug Report.* NSDUH = *National Survey on Drug Use and Health.* MTF = Monitoring the Future.

[a] UNODC (2009).

[b] UNODC (2010).

[c] SAMHSA (2002b, 2003, 2004, 2005, 2006, 2007b, 2008).

[d] Bachman, Johnston, and O'Malley (2005a, 2005b, 2008, 2009); Johnston, Bachman, and O'Malley (2003, 2005, 2006, 2009, 2010).

[e] There were important changes to the survey in 2002 that make it difficult to compare with earlier years.

[f] The difference in NSDUH estimates for 2007 and 2008 is not statistically significant (p-value = 0.2151).

fully responsible for these differences because it depends on data provided to it by member states, but more could be done to help researchers and policymakers understand how confident they should be in these figures.

As a final note of skepticism, consider a rough calculation of what the 2010 INCSR or WDR figure of 21,500 MT produced in 2008 would imply for U.S. consumption. After subtracting Mexican and southwest-border seizures (1,658 and 1,253 MT, respectively) and splitting across Mexico and the United States in proportion to their respective number of past-year users (10 percent/90 percent), this would suggest that U.S. consumption of Mexican marijuana is 16,730 MT, or a total consumption of 25,100 MT if one believes the 2006 WDR estimate that one-third of the U.S. marijuana market is supplied domestically. Even ignoring imports from Canada, Jamaica, and elsewhere, allowing for 20-percent underreporting in the household survey, and recognizing that past-month users account for 88 percent of reported past-year days of marijuana use, that combination suggests that, on average, those 15.2 million past-month users in the United States were each consuming approximately 1.2 kilograms (kg) of marijuana per year:

$$\frac{\dfrac{90\% \times \left(21{,}500\ \text{MT} - 1{,}658 - 1{,}253\ \text{per year}\right) \times 88\%}{1 - 33\%}}{\left(1 + 25\%\right) \times 15.2\ \text{million}} \approx 1.2\ \text{kg per year.}$$

That is just about enough for one joint every two hours for every waking hour of the year for every past-month user.

Note that the problem of supply-side estimates of marijuana production being high relative to demand-side estimates is not unique to Mexico and the United States; it is a global problem (Leggett, 2006).

The bottom line is that we should not place much faith in these supply-side estimates. There are problems and uncertainty in generating supply-side numbers, and the inability to apply consistent, evidence-based methods is a major limitation. That is why, when we estimate the size of the market, we rely on methods that have been verified in terms of their limitations (e.g., underreporting biases), and, in fact, a science is evolving regarding how to adjust for them.

Demand-Side Estimates

We also have important concerns about sizing drug markets based on demand-side estimates. Demand-side estimates start with counts of the numbers of people who consume drugs with various frequencies or intensities of use (e.g., occasional and hard-core, or daily, weekly, and past-year) and multiply those counts by average rates of consumption. One might adjust upward by some factor to account for underreporting in surveys, which is done even for surveys of the consumption of legal commodities (Cook, 2007).

The consumption figures generated this way look strong only relative to the supply-side estimates and not in any absolute sense. There are three main concerns:

- General population surveys (e.g., NSDUH) miss many heavy drug users who are in treatment, in jail or prison, or in an unstable housing situation; who are hard to locate; or who are unwilling to talk about their substance use.

- Respondents are not always accurate in their reports, either because of an intention to deceive or because they have trouble recalling details.
- There is limited evidence available about the amount of drugs consumed per use-day or session.

The first concern is not insurmountable as long as there is good source data with information about hard-to-reach populations that can complement the general population survey. Abt Associates (2001) and Pudney et al. (2006) provide good examples for how this can be done with information from arrestees and treatment populations. The second concern will always be an issue—one that requires analysts to use and justify credible inflation factors. (We address this in Chapter Three.) Finally, insights about amounts consumed can be obtained with information about expenditures and information about days of use and amount used per day. However, despite the large number of surveys that inquire about marijuana prevalence, there is almost no information about the amount and quality of what is typically consumed. As we demonstrate in the next section, even seemingly minor assumptions about amount consumed (e.g., the amount of marijuana in a joint) can have major impacts on total consumption estimates.

For estimates of DTO export revenue, this study relies primarily on demand-side estimates. This is sensible because Mexico plays a uniquely prominent role as a source and transshipment country for drugs coming into the United States (NDIC, 2010). (If the United States received substantial amounts from ten different countries, then uncertainty about the market share held by any one country would make any prorating of the market total to an individual country prohibitively speculative.)

Definitions and Distinctions

This section makes some useful distinctions to clarify thinking about how the Mexican DTOs generate money from producing and selling illicit drugs.

Revenues Versus Profits

Because drug trafficking does not involve many long-term capital investments, there is little gained from distinguishing between cash and accrual accounting principles. Nevertheless, net cash flow is different from (greater than) profits, at least as economists use the term. Much of drug dealers' apparent cash or "accounting" profit is not pure profit or "rent" in the economic sense; rather, it is compensation for the real but nonmonetary cost of various risks, including the risks of arrest, imprisonment, injury, and death (Reuter and Kleiman, 1986).

For some purposes, it is useful to label a portion of net revenues as risk compensation and focus on the remainder as true profits. We do not do that here, partly because such distinctions would overtax available data, but more fundamentally because of our interest in DTO violence. Plausibly, what fuels trafficking violence, corruption, and other ills is total revenues, not just economic profits.

Prices Along the Supply Chain

Most U.S. users do not buy directly from smugglers. Rather, those who carry drugs across the border typically sell to importers, who sell to wholesalers, who may sell to midlevel wholesalers or to retailers, who sell to users (see, e.g., Natarajan and Belanger, 1998). Prices rise at each step along that chain. For example, the kilogram of cocaine that costs $2,000 in Colombia and is worth $10,000 within Mexico might sell first in the United States for $14,000–$18,000 per kilogram but retail for the equivalent of $100,000–$150,000 per kilogram when broken down in $5 and $10 rocks of crack (see Appendix D, available online at http://www.rand.org/pubs/occasional_papers/OP325/).

Since these prices differ so much, it is useful to introduce some jargon. We define the *import price* as the first price paid for a shipment of drugs into the United States, and the *export price* as the price in Mexico for that same shipment. At the other end of the U.S. distribution chain, we refer to the price paid by the user as the *retail price*. There are a few complications, because some users barter goods (often stolen) or services (e.g., prostitution) instead of paying cash, but we defer such issues for now.

Since the distribution network in the United States has many layers, in theory, we would like to refer separately to the first-, second-, and *n*-level wholesale prices. In practice, data limitations constrain analysis to a single *wholesale price*, which is generally understood to be the price paid per kilogram (cocaine or heroin) or pound (in the case of marijuana). Because of price markups, the price per kilogram paid when importing bundles of 200 kg or more at a time is less than the price of a kilogram sold wholesale as a single kilogram. In practice, data are generally not available on the import price per se, so we instead use the wholesale price (price paid per kilogram or pound) in states in the American Southwest.

CHAPTER THREE

U.S. Marijuana Consumption and Mexican Drug-Trafficking Organizations' Revenues from Exporting Marijuana

To estimate gross revenues earned by Mexican DTOs from exporting marijuana to the United States, we estimate, in turn, (1) total U.S. marijuana consumption, (2) Mexican marijuana's market share, and (3) the price of Mexican marijuana at the wholesale level. Multiplying these three items generates our estimate of gross revenues earned through Mexican marijuana exports.

Total Consumption of Marijuana in the United States

Table 3.1 displays five demand-side estimates of the amount of marijuana consumed in the United States annually. As is clear, there is a lot of variation, with figures ranging over an order of magnitude from 1,000 MT to 5,000 MT, including one outlier estimate of 9,830 MT.

The estimates can become complicated in their details, but, at heart, they simply multiply the numbers of users estimated from general population surveys by the assumed rates of consumption per user, often broken down by user type. For example, Leggett (2006) suggests average consumption of 108 grams per past-year user;[1] the 2008 NSDUH estimates that there are 25.7 million past-year marijuana users; and a common guess of underreporting is 20 percent. Multiplying produces a point estimate of 25.7 million × 1.25 × 108 g = 3,470 MT

However, unpacking the 108 g figure underscores why uncertainty ranges can—and should—be so broad. As Table 3.2 shows, two-thirds of the past-year consumption is attributed to just 4 percent of heavy past-year users, and users in that 4 percent are assumed to consume at rates more than 100 times greater than the median past-year user. Past-year marijuana use is relatively common, so household surveys provide reasonably precise estimates. However, the number of chronic marijuana users, as defined by Leggett, is no greater than the number of heroin users. It is hard to rule out the possibility that the 4 percent should really be 2 percent or 6 percent, yet doing so would swing the total consumption estimate by ±33 percent.

It is likewise very hard to estimate the average grams consumed per year by any of these groups, but particularly for the chronic users. Most of these estimates are based on (1) self-reported days used per year (available from recent surveys), (2) joints consumed per use-day (based on household surveys from before 1995), and (3) estimates of the average joint size. Unfortunately, this question about number of joints consumed was removed from the household survey in 1994 and has not been repeated since then. The issue is also complicated by the

---

[1] This is consistent with other estimates in the literature (see discussions in Bouchard, 2007, and Kilmer and Pacula, 2009).

Table 3.1
Demand-Side Estimates of the Size of the U.S. Marijuana Market

Source	Year	User Estimate from the Household Survey	Approach for Calculating Amount Consumed	Amount (MT per year)
Abt Associates (2001)	2000	PM users in 2000 (12.1 million)	Joints per month, grams per joint	1,047
Kilmer and Pacula (2009)	2005	Separate estimates for two types of users: PM (14.6 million) and PY~PM (10.8 million). Best estimate assumed 20% underreporting.	Days per user, joints per day, grams per joint	2,950 (1,300–6,150)
DEA (DASC, 2002)	2000	11.7 million users[a]	Assumed 365 × 1 g for each user	4,270
UNODC (2009)[b]	2008	PY users in 2008 ages 15–64 (24.5 million)	Low and high estimates of annual consumption: 60 g and 200 g[c]	1,472–4,907
Gettman (2007)	2005	PY in 2005 (25 million). Assumed 40% underreporting.	Calculated with information about days per user (by gender), joints per day, grams per joint.	9,830

NOTE: PM = past month. PY = past year. PY~PM = past year but not in the past month. g = gram.

[a] We are unsure how this was generated, but it was listed as "Modified Consumption Estimate" based on Abt Associates (2001).

[b] UNODC provided a range for North America (1,876–6,252 MT), and we calculated the share attributable to the United States using data from the 2008 NSDUH.

[c] UNODC (2009) cites 2003 research by Van der Heijden and UNODC (2008) and states that neither source "differentiates between cannabis resin and herbal use" (UNODC, 2009, p. 92).

Table 3.2
Leggett's (2006) Typology of Past-Year Users and Associated Consumption Rates

Type	Percentage of Past-Year Users	Grams Used per Year	Percentage of Past-Year Grams Consumed
Casual	45	0.6	0.2
Regular	41	15	5.7
Daily	9	320	26.6
Chronic	4	1,825	67.5

NOTE: Totals may not sum to 100% due to rounding.

fact that marijuana is often used communally, with multiple people sharing one or more joints; moreover, some users do not consume marijuana as rolled joints.

Kilmer and Pacula (2009) recently reviewed the literature and settled on 0.4 g per joint as the best estimate. Relatively few of the estimates in the literature are based on original empirical analysis. An exception is Abt's (2001; see also Rhodes, 1995) estimate of 0.39 g per joint, which is derived from pre-1995 household survey data about (1) the amount used in the past month (either in joints or ounce categories) and (2) the number of days someone smoked in the past 30 days. Only one study reported an amount greater than 0.5 g per joint: Gettman's (2007) 0.75 g estimate. Gettman's (2007) estimate appears to be based on (1) the size of marijuana cigarettes created for those federal patients receiving marijuana from the University of

Mississippi (750 to 900 milligrams [mg], as cited in Azorlosa, Greenwald, and Stitzer, 1995) and (2) a training manual for California police officers that included information about the weights of various "types" of marijuana cigarettes but no information about the distribution of these joint sizes. Leggett (2006) reviews a variety of European studies that find substantially smaller joint sizes, but that is most likely attributable to the predominance of higher-potency sinsemilla in those markets.

As a contribution to this literature, Appendix A to this paper (available online at http://www.rand.org/pubs/occasional_papers/OP325/) examines purchases made by arrestees in the 2000–2003 Arrestee Drug Abuse Monitoring (ADAM) system. Comparing prices paid by those reporting having purchased one joint with prices paid by those purchasing 1 g, we estimate that a typical joint weighs about 0.46 g with a 95-percent confidence interval equal to 0.43–0.50 g. The applicability of this figure to other populations may be limited because ADAM is not representative of all U.S. arrestees, let alone of nonarrestees.

The other major question is how to adjust for survey respondents' underreporting their marijuana use. Kilmer and Pacula (2009) based its 20-percent underreporting estimate largely on Fendrich et al.'s (2004) study of a household population, which found that 78 percent of marijuana users self-reported their use. This was also consistent with the share of arrestees who self-reported their marijuana use in the 2003 ADAM (82 percent). A more recent assessment of arrestees in the 2008 ADAM data set also yielded a similar rate (82 percent; see ONDCP, 2009).

One reason the Gettman (2007) estimate of U.S. consumption is higher than the others is its assumption about underreporting. It is based on Harrison et al.'s (2007) finding that, among a sample of 12- to 24-year-olds in the 2001 NHSDA (the predecessor to NSDUH), 40 percent of those testing positive for marijuana did not report that they had used marijuana. However, the survey has since undergone changes that have improved the accuracy of reporting, including raising the response rate (SAMHSA, 2002b) and the study focused only on juveniles and young adults. For these reasons, we continue to assume 20-percent underreporting, but our upper-bound estimate of total consumption accommodates underreporting rates in excess of 40 percent.

There are a few reasons to believe that the 0.46 g–per-joint estimate from ADAM might be slightly inflated,[2] so we focus on the lower bound of the 95-percent confidence interval (0.43 g), which is very close to the figures used by Abt Associates (2001) and Kilmer and Pacula (2009). Using prevalence data from the 2008 NSDUH to update Kilmer and Pacula's (2009) estimate for 2005, this generates a total consumption figure of 3,268 MT, which we round to 3,300 MT. This is close to the midpoint of UNODC's (2009) estimate for 2008,

$$3,190 \text{ MT} = \frac{1,472 + 4,907}{2},$$

---

[2] See Appendix A, available online at http://www.rand.org/pubs/occasional_papers/OP325/.

although UNODC did not present this as a best estimate. There remains a lot of uncertainty about this figure, and alternative estimates will be considered in various sensitivity analyses reported in this paper.[3]

Mexican Marijuana's Share of the U.S. Market

In addition to uncertainty about the total size of the U.S. marijuana market, there is also considerable uncertainty about Mexican marijuana's share of that market. For our calculations, we assume that the share of U.S.-consumed marijuana that is imported from Mexico is in the range of 40 to 67 percent. This section explains why we believe this to be a reasonable estimate.

It is generally understood that most marijuana consumed in the United States is produced domestically or imported from Mexico, with smaller quantities being imported from Canada, Jamaica, and a few other minor suppliers.[4] However difficult it is to estimate total U.S. consumption, it is, in many respects, even harder to estimate market share by source. As noted in the U.S. Department of Justice's 2010 *National Drug Threat Assessment,*

> No reliable estimates are available regarding the amount of domestically cultivated or processed marijuana. The amount of marijuana available in the United States—including marijuana produced both domestically and internationally—is unknown. Moreover, estimates as to the extent of domestic cannabis cultivation are not feasible because of significant variability in or nonexistence of data regarding the number of cannabis plants not eradicated during eradication seasons, cannabis eradication effectiveness, and plant-yield estimates. (NDIC, 2010, "Drug Availability in the United States: Marijuana Availability," fn. 16)

The United Nations (UNODC, 2006) estimates that one-third of the cannabis consumed in the United States is produced domestically, up from one-sixth in the past, with an ongoing trend toward increasing proportions. Another estimate suggests that U.S. production accounts for half the market.[5] We do not know how these numbers were generated.

Another approach is to segment the market by price. High prices per gram are associated with high-potency forms of marijuana (sinsemilla—about 10–18 percent THC) produced pri-

---

[3] These calculations essentially convert all consumption into joint estimates, even though some consumers use different delivery mechanisms (e.g., bongs, one-hitters, edibles). Future work should examine the type of bias this assumption builds into this calculation, especially since some mechanisms, such as vaporizers, are believed to be much more efficient at extracting tetrahydrocannabinol (THC) (Abrams et al., 2007).

[4] It is very difficult to estimate the share of U.S.-consumed marijuana that comes from Canada. There are important disagreements in the scant literature about production, and many of the figures come from government sources without supporting documentation (Bouchard, 2008). It is believed that much of the marijuana imported from Canada is high-quality sinsemilla (e.g., BC Bud), but there are no hard numbers about the precise share. To the extent that Canada does export commercial-grade marijuana (marijuana that is neither sinsemilla nor ditchweed) into the United States, this would mean that our main estimates would overstate the Mexican DTO revenue from exporting marijuana into the United States.

[5] Rafael Fernández de Castro, who is the Presidential Advisor for International Affairs and Competitiveness, was attributed (Rios, 2010, p. 3, fn. 3) as saying, "Recent data has shown that 50% of the marijuana consumed in US is growth [sic] in American soil, principally in particular houses."

marily in the United States and Canada.[6] Low prices are associated with low- and midrange-potency marijuana. A large portion of this "commercial-grade" marijuana comes from Mexico (4–6 percent THC), although some is grown domestically. (See Appendix B, available online at http://www.rand.org/pubs/occasional_papers/OP325/, for more information about THC.)

There are two principal sources of user-reported prices that we can use to estimate the proportion of purchases that are of lower- versus higher-priced marijuana: NSDUH and ADAM. Both suggest that the price paid per gram or ounce in the majority of these purchases was well below the price of sinsemilla. Appendix C (available online at http://www.rand.org/pubs/occasional_papers/OP325/) describes the analysis in detail; although the proportions depend on user type, roughly 75–90 percent of the purchase prices were so low that they appear to have been for commercial grade, as opposed to sinsemilla, with 80 percent being perhaps a best guess.

The low proportion of purchases made at sinsemilla-like prices surprises us and seems at odds with the general world view obtained from descriptions of marijuana production and use available on the web or from marijuana advocacy organizations. However, it may be that medical marijuana is overrepresented in such discussions, and medical marijuana is almost all high-price, high-quality marijuana. Also, inasmuch as those writing for and reading the web tend to be more affluent and educated than most, it is important to remember that college graduates account for just 13 percent of reported days of marijuana use (SAMHSA, 2008). Thus, the world view reflected in the literature might not reflect a representative sample of marijuana users.

Having estimated how the U.S. marijuana market partitions into lower- versus higher-priced marijuana in the previous section, the next question is what Mexico's market share is in each of those segments. We believe that Mexico's market share is negligible in the higher-priced market segment because the great bulk of Mexico's exports are of commercial-grade marijuana. This is supported by the literature (e.g., ONDCP's Pulse Check, the National Drug Intelligence Center's [NDIC's] National Drug Threat Assessments).

While it may be tempting to use seizure data to help answer this question, we resist doing so for two reasons. First, and most obvious, we have no idea what the marijuana seizure rate is on either side of the border, and there is no reason to believe that it is the same. Second, there have been important changes in seizures on both sides of the border in recent years. In Mexico, the amount of cannabis eradicated dropped 50 percent from 2006 to 2008 (30,162 hectares and 15,756 hectares, respectively), because the military focused its attention on antiviolence measures instead of eradication (NDIC, 2010), not necessarily because production decreased. In the United States, the number of outdoor plants eradicated increased from 3 million in 2004 to 7.5 million in 2008, largely driven by an increase in seizures on federal lands (NDIC, 2010; the comparable figure for indoor plants seized for the entire country was 450,000 plants). What we do not know is how much of this is because of increased production on federal lands versus increased eradication efforts on federal lands, which would have increased the seizure rate. What we do know is that, throughout the 2001–2008 period, reported consumption in the United States remained amazingly stable (Table 2.1 in Chapter Two).

---

[6] According to DEA (NDIC, 2001c), "Sinsemilla, in Spanish, means without seed. Growing the female cannabis plant separate from the male cannabis plant prevents pollination, resulting in an increase in THC (tetrahydrocannabinol) levels and bud growth."

We think that it is noncontroversial to claim that at least 50 percent of the commercial-grade marijuana consumed in the United States comes from Mexico, especially because a number of law enforcement officials claim that the majority of marijuana consumed in their jurisdictions is from Mexico or is supplied by the Mexican DTOs (see Appendix E, available online at http://www.rand.org/pubs/occasional_papers/OP325/). This would suggest that at least 40 percent (50 percent × 80 percent) of the marijuana consumed in the United States comes from Mexico.

As for the upper bound for Mexican exports, we revisit the UNODC estimate that 33 percent of U.S. consumption is produced domestically. Based on our earlier analysis of the share of U.S. consumption that is sinsemilla, this UNODC number has face validity as a lower-bound estimate of the U.S. share. Our price analysis suggests that roughly 20 percent of the marijuana consumed in the United States is sinsemilla, which comes from the United States and, to a lesser extent, Canada. In our research for this report, we have not come across any claims that the majority of U.S. domestic production occurs indoors (indeed, no sources have suggested that this figure is even close.) Thus, the idea that *at least* 33 percent of the marijuana consumed in the United States comes from indoor and outdoor production in the United States seems credible. This suggests that an upper-bound estimate of the amount of total marijuana consumed in the United States that is imported from Mexico would be 67 percent (100 percent – 33 percent). Indeed, this is an upper bound because this figure also includes imports from other countries.

Recall the earlier quote from NDIC about the lack of reliable estimates of domestic production. Much more work could be done to improve these figures, and we highlight some ideas in the concluding chapter. Based on the arguments made in this section, we will assume that between 40 percent and 67 percent of the total marijuana consumed in the United States is imported from Mexico. Not only do we hope that these estimates are improved over time, but we also hope that readers realize that they might, in fact, change over time.

Wholesale Marijuana Prices Along the Southwest Border

Because most organizations that smuggle drugs across the U.S.–Mexican border are based in Mexico, it is not a bad approximation to assume that the entire markup from export to import

Table 3.3
Estimates of Wholesale Marijuana Prices Along the Southwestern U.S. Border, from Four Sources

Source	Year	Grade	Point Estimate ($/lb)	Range ($/lb)
NDIC[a]	Mostly 2001–2002	Mexican	400	300–500
Narcotic News[b]	2010	Commercial grade	397	250–500
STRIDE[c]	2005–2008	Not specified	323	234–334
ADAM[d]	2000–2003	Not specified	430	100–600

[a] NDIC (2001a, 2001b, 2002a, 2002b, 2007a, 2008a, 2008b, 2008c, 2008e).
[b] "Wholesale Marijuana Prices," undated.
[c] STRIDE = Drug Enforcement Administration, *System to Retrieve Evidence from Drug Evidence*, annual.
[d] Arrestee Drug Abuse Monitoring Program (2000, 2001, 2002, 2003).

price across that border accrues to Mexican DTOs. Certainly, there are some individuals and unaffiliated groups that smuggle small quantities across the border, but it is commonly believed that they hold a negligible market share, except perhaps for heroin (Díaz-Briseño, 2010; Quinones, 2010a, 2010b, 2010c).

We examined four data sources to generate an estimate of the wholesale marijuana prices along the southwestern border: NDIC, *Narcotic News*, DEA's STRIDE database, and ADAM. None of them is entirely satisfactory, but all are more or less in agreement; they have prices of $200–$500 per pound and tend to hover around $400 per pound (or $880 per kilogram; see Table 3.3). The data pertain to wholesale-level prices near the southwestern border, not import prices. However, inasmuch as Mexican DTOs vertically integrate into the wholesale market, these prices may give a better estimate of their revenues. See Appendix C (available online at http://www.rand.org/pubs/occasional_papers/OP325/) for additional information.

Table 3.4
Input Parameters Used to Generate Mexican Drug-Trafficking Organizations' Gross Revenues from Exporting Marijuana to the United States and Selling It to Wholesalers in the U.S. Southwest

	Low	Middle	High
Total U.S. consumption (MT)	1,500	3,300	4,900
Percentage imported from Mexico	40	54	67

NOTE: Low and high consumption estimates are from UNODC (2009). Middle consumption estimate is explained earlier in this chapter. The middle estimate for the share of U.S. consumption that comes from Mexico is the midpoint of the low and high estimates, which are explained earlier in this chapter.

Mexican Drug-Trafficking Organizations' Gross Revenues from Exporting Marijuana to the United States

Mexican DTOs' gross revenue from exporting marijuana to the border wholesale markets is simply total U.S. consumption multiplied by Mexican marijuana's market share multiplied by the wholesale price in border states.[7] To generate these estimates, we performed a simple Monte Carlo simulation using the parameters listed in Table 3.4 (10,000 trials, assuming triangle distribution for parameters). This yields an 80-percent confidence interval of $1.1 billion to $2 billion, with a best estimate close to $1.5 billion. U.S. marijuana consumption, as well as uncertainty about Mexico's market share, implies that the DTO revenues are best thought of as falling within a range, not as a single number. However, the entire span of this range is well below some of the figures mentioned in the literature, a point to which we return in Chapter Five.

---

[7] While we focus on gross export revenues here and in Chapter Five when we compare marijuana revenues to the revenues from other drugs, it would not be difficult to generate a good approximation of net revenues. First, it would require reducing the gross revenue figure by the product of the export price and amount exported (which is close to $80 per kilogram; see Appendix C, available online at http://www.rand.org/pubs/occasional_papers/OP325/). Second, it would require accounting for marijuana seized at the border and in Mexico that was owned by the DTOs. The former is easier to get than the latter (Appendix C), and it is unclear how important the latter is to these calculations. If one assumes that Mexico accounts for 2,000 MT of the marijuana consumed in the United States and another 1,500 MT is seized at the border, this suggests that we should reduce the gross revenues by $280 million (3,500,000 × $80) to generate a ballpark figure of net revenues.

CHAPTER FOUR

How Might Legalization in California Affect Mexican Drug-Trafficking Organizations' Marijuana Export Revenues?

Mexican DTOs earn $1.1 billion to $2 billion from exporting marijuana to the U.S. and selling it to wholesalers across the southwest border. Legalizing marijuana in California would present two sources of competition. The obvious one is marijuana sold legally in California to California residents and drug "tourists" visiting from out of state, as well as legalized home cultivation. A less obvious but potentially more important threat is marijuana diverted from legal distribution channels. The latter includes marijuana that is grown legally in California but then smuggled to another state and sold illegally there, as well as marijuana sold to underage users in California.

We believe that legalizing marijuana in California would effectively eliminate Mexican DTOs' revenues from supplying Mexican-grown marijuana to the California market. As we elaborate in this chapter, even with taxes, legally produced marijuana would likely cost no more than would illegal marijuana from Mexico and would cost less than half as much per unit of THC (Kilmer, Caulkins, Pacula, et al., 2010). Thus, the needs of the California market would be supplied by the new legal industry. While, in theory, some DTO employees might choose to work in the legal marijuana industry, they would not be able to generate unusual profits, nor be able to draw on talents that are particular to a criminal organization.

We also believe that Mexican DTOs would eventually lose all revenue stemming from the selling of Mexican marijuana to underage users in California. When it becomes possible in California for anyone over the age of 21 to provide juveniles with marijuana that is cheaper, better, and subject to more quality control, Mexican DTOs will have no more competitive advantage than they would trying to sell alcohol and cigarettes to California youth today.

The more interesting question is how much marijuana legally produced in California but then smuggled out of state would outcompete Mexican marijuana elsewhere in the country. We try to answer that question here.

Note that this analysis is predicated on an assumption that the federal government and the other states do not take effective measures to shut down those exports. If they do, then the overall answer is rather simple. California constitutes roughly one-seventh of the U.S marijuana market,[1] and the market share of domestically produced marijuana is generally believed to be higher in California than for the country as a whole, so one-seventh of $1.5 billion would constitute an upper bound on DTOs' revenue losses from export. That is, DTO losses would be small relative to their total drug revenues. The only way that California's marijuana legal-

---

[1] Combining census population data with the Substance Abuse and Mental Health Services Administration's (SAMHSA's) estimates of past-month marijuana prevalence by state (SAMHSA, 2007a) suggests that California has 13.5 percent of the past-month marijuana users living in the lower 48 U.S. states.

ization could substantially undercut DTO export revenues is if California marijuana diverted from legal production displaces Mexican marijuana elsewhere in the United States or if California establishes a precedent that leads to the legalization of marijuana in other states.

Kilmer, Caulkins, Pacula, et al. (2010) developed a model of postlegalization production costs assuming that the threat of federal enforcement limited production to grow houses. They relied on data from a variety of grey and standard literature sources, including DEA (1993) and Toonen, Ribot, and Thissen (2006). Their model's 80-percent confidence interval for the untaxed price was $330–$480 per pound of sinsemilla, with a best guess of $400 per pound.[2]

Note that this would be the price for sinsemilla, which is a high-potency form of marijuana, with THC content typically in the range of 10–18 percent. In contrast, the typical THC content of Mexican imports is 4–6 percent (see Appendix B, available online at http://www.rand.org/pubs/occasional_papers/OP325/).[3] Legal sales would incur the standard sales tax plus, in all likelihood, some sort of excise tax.

Proposition 19 does not specify a tax rate, leaving it to the more than 500 individual cities and counties to set their own rates. This could well set off a "race-to-the-bottom" competition among municipalities to charge low taxes to win the other benefits of hosting the industry (e.g., jobs, property taxes, sales taxes from drug tourism). However, even if there were a $25-per-ounce excise tax, that would still leave the price of legal sinsemilla around $60–$75 per ounce, including taxes, distribution costs, and a 20- to 50-percent retail markup. That is similar to the current price for Mexican marijuana in California (NDIC, 2008c).[4]

If consumers have a choice between black-market Mexican commercial-grade marijuana and legal sinsemilla that is 2–3.6 times more potent at the same cost, we presume that essentially all consumers in California would prefer to buy the legally produced California sinsemilla.

But what would happen in a state other than California, such as Wisconsin? Two sources of information suggest that, currently, Mexican marijuana sells in Wisconsin for about $1,075 per pound at the wholesale level ("Wholesale Marijuana Prices," undated; NDIC, undated).[5]

---

[2]   This is for unbranded sinsemilla that is not bundled with other goods or services (i.e., not impregnated in, for instance, brownies or beer and not for on-site consumption). The production model imagined a typical residential house essentially filled with 1,300 square feet of hydroponic growing under artificial lights, producing four harvests per year with a total yield of a little less than 550 pounds of sinsemilla per year. Allowing for one full-time agricultural worker to tend the plants and others to do the processing, aided by automation at the high end of what is available for marijuana today (which is very much at the low end relative to conventional food processing technology), Kilmer, Caulkins, Pacula, et al. (2010) estimate production costs of $200–$400 per pound with additional processing costs of $20–$35 per pound and a 6- to 40-percent markup. Assuming that an entrepreneur ran 10–20 houses, that markup of roughly $500,000–$750,000 would be sufficient to cover normal profit, consulting time of a master grower training and guiding the laborers, and back-office operations (e.g., bookkeeping, sales).

[3]   If federal law enforcement were so laissez-faire that it were possible to farm marijuana outdoors, then outdoor production would be cheaper per unit of THC than the grow-house model, even if the outdoor marijuana were not sinsemilla. Indeed, imported illegal Mexican marijuana would have a very hard time competing with marijuana that is farmed outdoors legally almost regardless of the excise tax or domestic smuggling cost.

[4]   The Los Angeles County Regional Criminal Information Clearinghouse (CLEAR) quotes a slightly higher price of $75–$100 per ounce for Mexican marijuana (CLEAR, 2007).

[5]   The sources are the *Narcotic News* website and NDIC market analyses. Their prices are highly correlated but do not appear to be copying the same source material; for only one state do they quote exactly the same price (Utah, $600–$1,000 per pound). We ultimately used the *Narcotic News* data for reasons explained in Appendix C (available online at http://www.rand.org/pubs/occasional_papers/OP325/).

Suppose that someone diverted legally produced sinsemilla at the wholesale level, after a $25-per-ounce excise and a 9-percent sales tax had been collected, raising the price from $400 to $836 per pound. It is roughly 1,750 miles from Humboldt County, California (a major marijuana production hub), to Wisconsin. Bond and Caulkins (2010) examined the current price gradient by which marijuana prices rise with distance from the source in the United States; their point estimate is $450 per pound per thousand miles.[6] At a $450-per-pound-per-thousand-mile rate, diverted California sinsemilla would cost $836 + $450 × 1.75, or roughly $1,625 per pound in Wisconsin.

So, one guess is that sinsemilla diverted from legal California production might cost 1.5 times as much per pound in Wisconsin as Mexican marijuana now does, but it would also be 2–3.6 times more potent, so the cost per unit of THC or per hour of intoxication would be lower. To the best of our knowledge, no one has studied empirically how marijuana consumers trade off price and potency. We carry through the calculations assuming that it is price per unit of THC that matters most, but we vary the potency ratio parameter and recognize that other considerations could matter outside of these calculations.

We replicated this analysis for the other 47 states (including the District of Columbia) in the lower 48. The result was that diverted California sinsemilla would be cheaper, per unit of THC, than the current Mexican marijuana price in every state except New Mexico and Texas. Since New Mexico and Texas together have just 6.6 percent of the past-month marijuana users living in the lower 48 states, this suggests that California's legalizing marijuana might take away more like 95 percent of the Mexican DTOs' U.S. marijuana market, not just California's share (one-seventh; SAMHSA, 2008).[7]

There are, however, uncertain parameters in the calculation above—notably,

- whether excise taxes are paid on diverted marijuana and, if so, at what rate
- the precise cost of smuggling-diverted marijuana across the United States
- how consumers perceive the potency differential (i.e., how many grams of Mexican marijuana is one gram of sinsemilla worth?)
- by how much California sinsemilla must undercut current prices—after adjusting for the difference in potency—to capture market share from Mexican marijuana (after all, if the California sinsemilla were cheaper by the potency-adjusted equivalent of only 5 percent, dealers of Mexican marijuana might simply cut their prices by 10 percent).

This is not an exhaustive list. For example, there is also uncertainty about the current price of Mexican marijuana and about the California production cost. Nevertheless, the four issues just named are the most consequential.

We deal with the last item by plotting a reverse cumulative distribution of the proportion of marijuana users in the lower 48 states for whom the potency-adjusted price would fall by

---

[6]   The estimate was based on the pronounced gradient in Mexican marijuana prices, with prices increasing with distance from Mexico. The relationship was observed in four different data sets, two from law enforcement and two from user self-report ("Marijuana Prices in the U.S.A., [undated], DEA's *Illegal Drug Price/Purity Reports* [IDPPRs] [DEA, annual], the ADAM system [ADAM, 1987–2003], and the 1996-2005 Trans High Market Quotations from *High Times* magazine).

[7]   Sinsemilla diverted from legal California production would be an even more effective competitor to current illicit sinsemilla suppliers. California sinsemilla would take over essentially the entire U.S. sinsemilla market. But that is not a concern to Mexican DTOs, which do not currently compete extensively in that market.

a given percentage. Figure 4.1 shows the plot for the parameter values used in the Wisconsin example above. For now, focus only on the middle of the three curves.

To read this graph, note that it includes a point whose coordinates are 50 percent on the horizontal axis and 19 percent on the vertical axis. That means that 19 percent of past-month users in the lower 48 states would enjoy a price decline of 50 percent or more relative to what they are now paying for Mexican marijuana. The median user (50 percent on the vertical axis) would enjoy a potency-adjusted price decline of about 38 percent (middle curve reaches 50 percent at a horizontal-axis value of 38 percent).

The other two lines show how this curve would shift if the smuggling costs were $300 and $600 per pound per thousand miles, respectively.[8] Reducing the smuggling cost from $450 to $300 per pound shifts the curve to the right and so only reinforces the base-case conclusion that Mexican DTOs would lose the great majority of their market share. However, if the smuggling cost were $600 per pound per thousand miles (left-most curve), then the potency-equivalent price would fall for only 85 percent of past-month marijuana users. This assumes the marijuana is diverted after taxes are collected; prices would still fall everywhere except Texas if the diversion occurred pretax. The same would hold if federal enforcement within California were so lax that marijuana could be farmed outdoors.

Figure 4.1
Proportion of Past-Month Marijuana Users in the Lower 48 States for Whom Potency-Adjusted Marijuana Prices Would Fall by a Given Amount

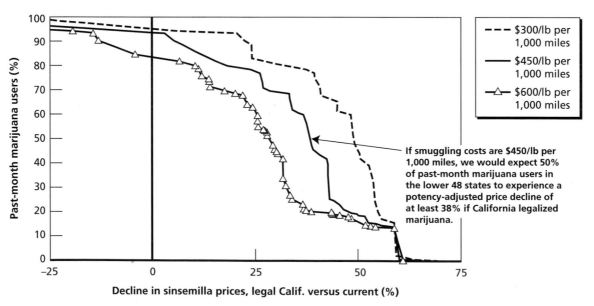

NOTE: Assumes $25-per-ounce excise tax and a potency equivalence ratio of 2.8:1.
RAND OP325-4.1

---

[8]   Bond and Caulkins (2010) report the range as $300–$1,000 to include the one estimate (based on ADAM) that was close to $1,000. However, the $1,000 figure is not credible in this context. More than 60 percent of past-month marijuana users live in states where the cost of Mexican marijuana (in dollars per pound) is less than the distance from Mexico (in miles). That is, the current price of Mexican marijuana would not be high enough with the $1,000 figure to cover even the smuggling costs within the United States, let alone the costs of acquiring the marijuana and smuggling into the United States across the U.S.-Mexico international border.

Figure 4.2 provides the corresponding sensitivity analysis with respect to the number of grams of Mexican marijuana that consumers deem to be worth as much as 1 g of sinsemilla from California. We vary this parameter over the range we reported above for the potency ratio (2–3.6), but other factors could come into play. Some might prefer a less intense high and be willing to pay more per unit of THC for Mexican marijuana; others might be willing to pay a premium per unit of THC for marijuana diverted from legal production because it is perceived to be safer or more uniform in quality.

Varying this potency parameter matters more. If 1 g of sinsemilla is judged to be as valuable as only 2 g of Mexican marijuana, not 2.8, then California sinsemilla would undercut the Mexican marijuana price for only 70 percent of past-month users. (The proportion rises to 89 percent if the sinsemilla is diverted from legal California production before sales and excise taxes are collected.)

The effect of the excise tax being $50 per ounce, not just $25 per ounce, is intermediate between that of having a higher smuggling cost or a lower potency-equivalence ratio, so we do not show that graph.

So far, we have not talked about one detail. Mexican marijuana's market share is not the same throughout the United States. It appears to be particularly low in the Appalachian region, where there is more domestic production (NDIC, 2007b). More generally, Mexican marijuana's market share may decrease as one moves north, away from Mexico, as might be expected, since smuggling costs rise with distance.

If the sinsemilla diverted from California production undercut current prices primarily in places where Mexican marijuana has modest market share, then California's legalization could have a smaller effect than just projected.

Figure 4.2
Proportion of Past-Month Marijuana Users in the Lower 48 States for Whom Potency-Adjusted Marijuana Prices Would Fall by a Given Amount, Relative to Current Mexican-Marijuana Prices

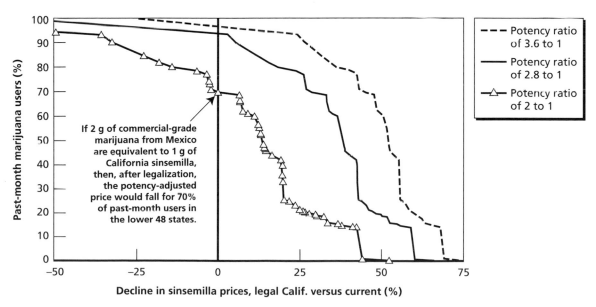

NOTE: Assumes $25-per-ounce excise tax and smuggling costs of $450 per pound per thousand miles.
RAND OP325-4.2

We do not have detailed data on state-by-state market share of Mexican marijuana. (Appendix E, available online at http://www.rand.org/pubs/occasional_papers/OP325/, collects pertinent information, but it is qualitative.) As a crude proxy, we replicated the analysis above but with Mexican marijuana's market share decreasing linearly with distance from Mexico, with a slope chosen to yield a particular overall national market share. We then varied that slope and associated national market share, and observed whether that affected the results above. When the slope is 0, we get exactly the results above because Mexican marijuana's relative share is the same throughout the lower 48 states. When the slope is very steep, Mexican sales are modeled as being concentrated in the part of the United States that is close to Mexico.

Not surprisingly, the more concentrated Mexican marijuana's sales are along the Mexican border, the less vulnerable they are to California marijuana legalization. However, at least when modeled in this way, the effect turns out to be very modest. The marijuana exported by Mexican DTOs essentially always dominates the New Mexico and Texas markets but loses the California market and points farther north (Oregon and Washington). There is a large section of the country (by area) where there are some distance interactions, but those Great Plains and Rocky Mountain states are sparsely populated and so, in comparison to more-populated states, do not have a lot of marijuana users. Most of the rest of the U.S. population is east of the Mississippi, and creating heterogeneous market shares that shift users of Mexican marijuana closer to Mexico also tends to bring them closer to California, reducing smuggling costs for the California sinsemilla.

Figure 4.3 has four lines corresponding to four scenarios with respect to the other parameters. The lowest line is our base case, under which Mexican marijuana retains less than 9–15 percent of its original market share. The line above the base-case line shows that, with a $600-per-pound-per-thousand-mile smuggling cost, Mexican marijuana would retain 20–26 percent of its market share. The third line shows that, with a $50- instead of $25-per-ounce excise tax, Mexican marijuana would retain 25–33 percent of its market share. The top line shows that, if 1 g of sinsemilla were valued as 2 g (instead of 2.8 g) of Mexican marijuana, the share increases to 33–38 percent.

However, for present purposes, the central point is that all four lines are fairly flat. Details about the distribution of Mexican-marijuana consumption within the United States do not matter much, at least as modeled here. Rather, it is the values of the parameters presented here that matter more, as indicated by the large vertical gaps between the four (more or less horizontal) lines.

In summary, our best guess is that legalizing marijuana production in California would wipe out essentially all DTO marijuana revenues from selling Mexican marijuana to California users; however, the share of Mexican marijuana in the United States that comes from Mexico to California is no more than one-seventh of all Mexican imports. If the federal government reacted to Prop 19 in a fairly passive way, sinsemilla diverted from legal California production and smuggled out of state could undercut current Mexican-marijuana prices on a per-unit-THC basis everywhere except Texas and New Mexico, thereby eliminating the vast majority of the U.S. market for illegal Mexican marijuana. (This assumes that interstate smuggling costs matched the current gradient in marijuana prices observed within the United States, with increasing distance from its source.) We reach that conclusion even with some conservative assumptions, notably including that a 9-percent sales tax and a $25-per-ounce excise tax will be collected before the sinsemilla is diverted.

Figure 4.3
Proportion of Current Mexican-Marijuana Sales That Would Not Be Undercut by Diverted California Sinsemilla

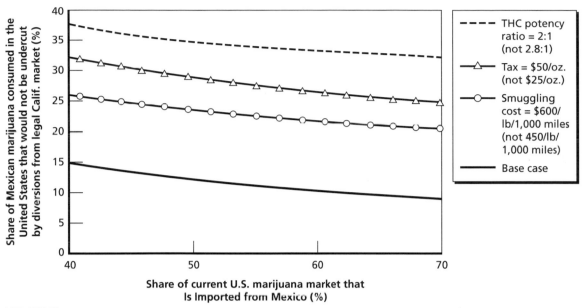

RAND OP325-4.3

It is important to stress that any projection related to drug legalization is subject to great uncertainty. Uncertainty can come from things outside the scope of these calculations. For example, if California implemented a tightly controlled legalization that made diversion very difficult, the results would be different. Likewise, if Mexican marijuana producers and smugglers could easily cut their current prices substantially, they might retain market share and do so against a market that was even larger in terms of amount, although perhaps not in terms of dollar value.

There is also uncertainty in the parameter values—notably, the number of grams of Mexican marijuana that consumers would view as equivalent to 1 g of sinsemilla diverted from legal California production. Hence, in the Monte Carlo simulation below, we allow for the cut in Mexican DTOs' marijuana export revenues to vary between 65 percent and 90 percent, but we keep 85 percent as the most likely reduction. As a reminder, that aspect of the simulation applies only if the federal government and other states do not or cannot block California marijuana from supplying the other states. If marijuana produced legally stays in California, then we do not need a simulation to estimate the proportion of DTO marijuana export revenues that would be lost. It is essentially just 14 percent, because that is California's approximate share (one-seventh) of current U.S. marijuana consumption.

We suggest viewing these two projections (65–90 percent and 14 percent) as two separate conditional projections—specifically, as projections conditional on the federal response—not as lower and upper ends of a continuous range over which one might seek some average.

We do not believe that the federal government will stand idly by if California were to capture the entire national market now held by Mexico-sourced marijuana. It would be difficult not to notice that the quantities produced and perhaps even taxed were vastly larger than what is needed to supply the California market alone. However, we cannot predict what or how effective the federal government's reaction might be. It is not difficult to imagine ways in which the federal government, perhaps spurred on by other states, might provide California incentives to crack down on diversion. For example, withholding federal highway funds would more than likely offset any marijuana tax revenues, making marijuana legalization a budget problem, not a budget rescue. However, voter-passed propositions are not easy to repeal, and Prop 19 places regulatory authority primarily in the hands of the separate county and municipal governments, not the state. So even if the federal government "punishes" California in some way for legalizing marijuana, it could take some time for California to develop and impose effective controls. How the issue of politics and federalism plays out is not something we can model; nor is it something about which we have unique expertise. However, we can only point out that the only scenario under which California's legalizing marijuana can possibly have a noteworthy impact on DTOs' drug revenues requires the federal government to respond in ways that some might not find acceptable.

CHAPTER FIVE

Beyond Marijuana Exports: Insights About Additional Sources of Mexican Drug-Trafficking Organizations' Drug Revenue

Mexican DTOs generate revenue from a host of drugs, products, and services; in other words, exporting marijuana to the United States is only part of the portfolio. This chapter provides a critical assessment of the claim that 60 percent of Mexican DTO drug revenues come from marijuana and presents an exploratory analysis of DTO revenues from exporting other drugs. It concludes with a discussion about DTO revenues from domestic distribution within the United States.

Assessing the Claim That 60 Percent of Mexican Drug-Trafficking Organization Drug Revenues Are from Marijuana

Background

It is common in contentious policy domains for sensational numbers to get the most attention and to be repeated so often that they take on an aura of undeserved credibility (Reuter, 1984; Best, 2001). Thus, it is not surprising that much attention has been given to the claim that 60 percent of DTO drug revenues come from marijuana, implying that the DTOs generate more money from marijuana than from all the other substances *combined*. Interestingly, this seems to be one of the few figures on which advocates on both sides of the debate agree.[1] This ubiquitous figure was created by government sources, and it is regularly used by those seeking to legalize marijuana.

These figures, reproduced in Table 5.1, were first published in ONDCP's 2006 *National Drug Control Strategy* (NDCS) with the following accompanying text:

> The US Government estimates that Mexican traffickers receive more than $13.8 billion in revenue from illicit-drug sales to the United States; 61 percent of that revenue, or $8.5 billion, is directly tied to marijuana export sales. Marijuana has become the primary revenue source for Mexican drug trafficking organizations, eclipsing the potential revenue from cocaine, heroin, and methamphetamine combined. . . . (p. 36)

The sources for these numbers were listed as NDIC and ONDCP, but none of the calculations underlying them was included. The remainder of this section explains why we are skeptical of this 60 percent claim, and it is important to note that in September 2010, ONDCP publicly distanced itself from this figure (Hamsher, 2010; ONDCP, 2010b).

---

[1] In the case of drug revenues, both sides of the debate on legalization benefit from large numbers; legalization proponents use them to show that the problem is large, while those opposed use them to illustrate the drug's dangers to society.

Table 5.1
Revenue Estimates for Mexican Drug-Trafficking Organizations from the Office of National Drug Control Policy and National Drug Intelligence Center, c. 2005

Drug	Amount ($ billions)	Share of Drug Revenues (%)
Marijuana	8.57	61.7
Cocaine	3.96	28.5
Methamphetamine	1.02	7.3
Heroin	0.34	2.5
Total	13.89	100

SOURCE: ONDCP (2006, p. 36).

NOTE: A year was not given, but the data were published in the 2006 strategy. A news story featuring former ONDCP director John P. Walters in 2008 mentioned the estimate as for 2004–2005, and the reporter noted, "These are the only figures available, because this was the first time the agency conducted a market analysis, a spokesman said" (Corchado, 2008).

There Is No Empirical Justification for This Figure That Can Be Verified

We are not aware of any publicly available documents that provide empirical support for these figures. Not only does this make it difficult to assess whether the figures are correct; it also makes it difficult to understand what these figures actually cover. The chart was titled "Estimated Revenue for Mexican Drug Trafficking Organizations," which could mean total revenue, net revenue, or net export revenue. The reference to $8.57 billion for marijuana being "directly tied to marijuana export sales" suggests that this is an export revenue figure, which would not be surprising because it is very difficult to estimate domestic distribution revenues.

Subsequent National Drug Intelligence Center Estimates Reveal Large Uncertainty About These Numbers

After these figures were published in 2006, an August 2007 U.S. Government Accountability Office (GAO) (GAO, 2007) report published a different set of figures from NDIC for 2005. This time the figures were presented as ranges, not as point estimates:

> According to the National Drug Intelligence Center, drug proceeds in Mexico in 2005 ranged from $2.9 billion to $6.2 billion for cocaine (including Central America), $324 million to $736 million for heroin, $3.9 billion to $14.3 billion for marijuana, and $794 million to $1.9 billion for methamphetamine. Mexican drug traffickers also grow marijuana in the United States; therefore, the amount of proceeds returned to Mexico is likely greater than the reported estimates. (p. 13)

It is unclear whether these ranges were generated from the same process that yielded the figures that were published in the 2006 NDCS (ONDCP, 2006). (NDIC was listed as a source for both.) The 2006 NDCS numbers are not the midpoints for the ranges in the GAO 2007 figures, but they are included in them.

The most striking range is the one for marijuana: $3.9 billion to $14.3 billion. Just to put this uncertainty in perspective, this difference of $10.4 billion is roughly *double* the total revenue reported for the three other drugs reported in the 2006 NDCS. The quote also provides circumstantial support for the conjecture that the 2006 NDCS figure did not include revenues from Mexican DTOs growing marijuana within the United States, but there is no way to verify this.

The $8.57 Billion Figure for Drug-Trafficking Organizations' Marijuana Revenues Is Not Credible

A simple calculation shows that the original $8.57 billion figure in the 2006 NDCS is implausible. Appendix C (available online at http://www.rand.org/pubs/occasional_papers/OP325/) suggests that wholesale (U.S.) prices for marijuana near the Mexican border did not change much throughout the decade. Dividing the $8.57 billion by the $880-per-kilogram wholesale price implies that in excess of 9,700 MT of Mexican marijuana made it to wholesalers in the United States. That is roughly *double* the size of UNODC's high estimate and almost *three times* our estimate of 3,300 MT.

Also, as noted above, this includes only Mexican marijuana. Earlier, we suggested that Mexican marijuana accounts for, at most, 67 percent of the marijuana consumed in the United States, so the $8.57 billion figure indirectly implies that the United States consumed at least 14,500 MT circa 2005. Allowing for 20-percent underreporting in the household survey and recognizing that past-month users account for 88 percent of reported past-year days of marijuana use, that combination suggests that, on average, those 14.6 million past-month users in the United States (see Table 2.1 in Chapter Two) were each consuming about 700 g of marijuana per year:

$$\frac{14,500 \text{ MT} \times 88\%}{(1+25\%) \times 14.6 \text{ million}} \approx 700 \text{ g/year}.$$

That is almost 4.5 joints per day for *every* past-month user for *every* day of the year. Since some of this marijuana is seized after it gets past the southwestern U.S. border, the actual figure would be lower than 4.5 joints per day every day; however, the seizure rate would have to be unrealistically high to make these numbers credible.

This 60-percent figure is truly a mythical number, one that appeared out of nowhere and that has acquired great authority (Singer, 1971; Reuter, 1984). This figure should not be taken seriously.

Exploratory Analysis of Gross Export Revenues for Other Drugs

We sought to estimate DTOs' revenues from other substances so as to calculate the share of their drug export revenues that can be attributed to marijuana. This is a preliminary exercise, because data on some important parameters are weak,[2] including the share of Colombian heroin that is trafficked by the Mexican DTOs. We focus on *gross* revenues because estimating *net* revenues requires information about what DTOs pay to produce or purchase the drugs; the

---

[2] Compared with marijuana, the household and student surveys provide much less useful information for cocaine/crack, heroin, and methamphetamine. Estimates depend on a variety of other sources, such as the ADAM program and the *Treatment Episode Data Set* (TEDS).

quality of publicly available information on these parameters is not good enough to support even preliminary calculations.

We estimate Mexican DTOs' gross export revenues for cocaine, heroin, and methamphetamine as follows. For each substance, dividing the national retail market value by the retail price per pure kilogram (1,000 × price per pure gram) gives pure kilograms consumed. Dividing by wholesale purity converts to total kilograms imported at the actual wholesale purity. Multiplying by the wholesale price at the border yields total export revenues for all exporters, Mexican and other. Finally, multiplying by the share of the drug believed to come from or through Mexico gives an estimate of Mexican DTO export revenues for that drug.

To give a specific example, if U.S. consumers spent $30 billion on cocaine at an average retail price of $145 per pure gram, that implies consumption of 207 pure metric tons, which is the equivalent of 252 MT at the typical purity of 82 percent seen along the border. Multiplying by a wholesale price along the southwestern U.S. border of $17,000 per kilogram suggests that total cocaine export revenues are $4.3 billion per year. If Mexican DTOs smuggle 80 percent of that, their revenues are $3.4 billion per year. Table 5.2 repeats the arithmetic for the other three substances using point estimates for the parameters. Appendix D (available online at http://www.rand.org/pubs/occasional_papers/OP325/) explains the empirical basis for the parameter estimates and provides associated ranges.

Given that we have criticized others for not clearly stating their confidence in the figures they publish, we would be remiss if we did not acknowledge the great uncertainty surrounding these figures. We partially address this by considering ranges (see Appendix D) and by using Monte Carlo analysis, but this does not account for the fact that we have very little information about the size of the U.S. methamphetamine market (see Nicosia et al., 2009), and we do

Table 5.2
Exploratory Point Estimates of Mexican Drug-Trafficking Organizations' Export Revenues from Other Drugs

Estimate Point	Cocaine	Mexican Heroin	Colombian Heroin	Meth
Value of U.S. market at retail ($ billions)	30	10	10	5
Retail price per pure kilogram (1,000 × price per pure gram)	145,000	450,000	450,000	260,000
Implied consumption in pure metric tons	207	22	22	19
Purity at wholesale/import level (%)	82	35	60	75
Implied consumption at wholesale purity (MT)	252	64	37	26
Import price per kilogram (not adjusted for purity) ($)	17,000	22,500	60,000	30,865
Total export revenues of all traffickers ($ billions)	4.3	1.4	2.2	0.8
U.S. market share exported from Mexico (%)	80	30[a]	30[b]	77.5
Export revenues of Mexican DTOs ($ billions)	3.4	0.4	0.7	0.6

NOTE: See Appendix D, available online at http://www.rand.org/pubs/occasional_papers/OP325/, for the ranges considered for these estimates.

[a] This point estimate suggests that 30 percent of heroin consumed in the United States is produced in Mexico.

[b] This point estimate suggests that 30 percent of heroin consumed in the United States is produced in Colombia and smuggled through Mexico.

not know how much Colombian heroin is smuggled into the United States through Mexican DTOs. We include these preliminary estimates in part because they shed some light on the current question. It is our hope that, over time, these figures will be refined, by ourselves and others, thus helping to provide more-precise estimates down the road.

For the Monte Carlo simulation, we treat the parameters as random variables with a triangle distribution, so they can take on any value between their low and high values but are most likely to be near the base values. (See Appendix D for ranges.) We generate 10,000 trial estimates of the gross export revenues for marijuana, cocaine, heroin, and methamphetamine and the proportion of marijuana revenues that would be lost. For each trial, we then determine what proportion of gross export revenue from drugs the DTOs (1) now obtain from marijuana and (2) would lose if marijuana were legalized in California (assuming that California marijuana were diverted to other states, to the extent described in Chapter Four).

As noted earlier, eighty percent of the trial results have revenue losses between 13 percent and 23 percent, with the median value being an 18-percent reduction in DTOs' gross drug revenues. The corresponding distribution for current share of revenues is slightly larger (a range of 15–26 percent, with a median of 20 percent), but only slightly higher because the projection in Chapter Four involves California marijuana outcompeting Mexican imports throughout most of the United States. Needless to say, our range of 15–26 percent is much smaller than the oft-quoted (see, e.g., ONDCP, 2006; Fainaru and Booth, 2009; Yes on 19, undated) 60-percent number.

The reason, in a nutshell, is differences in estimates of marijuana revenues. Our point estimate of gross revenues from the other three drugs (cocaine, heroin, and methamphetamine) obtained by summing across the last row of Table 5.2 was $5.1 billion; the corresponding total from ONDCP (2006) is $5.3 billion. The match is not exact. ONDCP's heroin figure looks more like our figure of what Mexican DTOs make just from Mexican heroin, without counting revenues from Colombian heroin transshipped through Mexico. Conversely, ONDCP's methamphetamine figure is higher, which makes sense, because it pertains to 2005, which was probably the peak year for methamphetamine.[3] From the perspective of estimating marijuana's share of revenues, however, these differences are minor and offset by other parameters. We and ONDCP (2006) agree on the total for the other three drugs (Mexican heroin, Colombian heroin, and methamphetamine) and on the fact that cocaine is by far the biggest revenue generator among the three.

Again, where we differ is with the marijuana estimate. The ONDCP (2006) figure was $8.57 billion. Eighty percent of the trial results from the Monte Carlo simulation suggest gross marijuana export revenues between $1.1 billion and $2 billion.

---

[3] Given the previously mentioned difficulties of tracking methamphetamine use, it is difficult to know precisely when consumption peaked; however, a number of sources suggest that it was close to 2005. Treatment admissions for which methamphetamine was the primary substance peaked in 2005 (TEDS) and felony arrests for dangerous drugs (which largely consists of methamphetamine) in California peaked in 2005 (CJCS, 2008).

Drug-Trafficking Organizations' Revenues from Domestic Distribution Within the United States

Aside from moving marijuana and other drugs across the border, the Mexican DTOs generate revenue by participating in the domestic distribution of these substances (NDIC, 2010, 2008e). There are also reports that these DTOs are involved in producing methamphetamine and marijuana in the United States (the latter reportedly in national parks), but there is little hard evidence about the extent of Mexican DTO production, at least in part because the workers on site "have no idea who they are working for and are able to give little information when arrested" (Fainaru and Booth, 2009).

We have already included in our DTO revenue estimates some part of what formally is domestic markup. Our "import" prices are really wholesale prices in the Southwest, so we have already given the DTOs "credit" for controlling and deriving revenues from sales down to that level.

It is not at all clear how much more vertically integrated the DTOs are down the distribution chain within the United States. The 2007 *National Drug Threat Assessment* (NDIC, 2007d, as quoted in GAO, 2007) reports that, "although [Mexican] DTOs tend to be less structured in the United States than in Mexico, they have regional managers throughout the country and rely on Mexican street gangs to distribute illicit drugs at the retail level" (p. 18). Based on prison-inmate surveys, Mexicans and Mexican-Americans do not dominate drug distribution in the United States; in 2004, they accounted for just 4 percent and 8 percent, respectively, of people imprisoned in the United States for drug distribution (Caulkins and Sevigny, 2010).

However, Mexicans do play a role in the subsequent distribution beyond import; those imprisoned include respondents who describe themselves as wholesale and retail sellers, not just importers or couriers (Caulkins and Sevigny, 2010). Ethnographic studies, such as Hoffer's (2006) analysis of Denver's heroin markets report Mexican dealers arriving by bus from the border, bringing in small quantities of heroin, not only large import lots.[4]

Unfortunately, even if we somehow knew what proportion of the domestic markup was captured by Mexican nationals, that would not tell us much about DTO revenues from foreign operations in the United States. Presumably, many Mexican nationals who sell drugs in the United States are not affiliated with any of the DTOs. In fact, 90 percent of Mexican-American and 94 percent of Mexican nationals imprisoned in the United States for drug selling report no organizational affiliation (Caulkins and Sevigny, 2010).

As noted earlier, it is very difficult to calculate the overall effect of marijuana legalization on the Mexican DTOs because we neither know the extent of their current involvement in the domestic marijuana trade in the United States nor the role they would play in smuggling California sinsemilla to other states postlegalization.

Concluding Thoughts

The ubiquitous claim that 60 percent of Mexican DTO export revenues come from U.S. marijuana consumption is not credible. Our exploratory analysis of gross export revenues suggests

---

[4]   A series of articles in the *Los Angeles Times* also told the story of how small heroin networks from Xalisco were supplying many midsized cities with heroin and providing excellent customer service (Quinones, 2010a, 2010b, 2010c).

that marijuana accounts for a smaller share (15–26 percent), but inferences are limited because the evidence base for cocaine, heroin, and methamphetamine is small (especially for the latter; see Appendix D, available online at http://www.rand.org/pubs/occasional_papers/OP325/, for more info).

As mentioned in the previous section, the DTOs make money not only from moving product across the border to wholesalers but also from distributing the drugs throughout the United States (and, in some cases, even from producing them). The extent to which the Mexican DTO members are involved depends on location and drug. Future work should focus on estimating the revenues from domestic distribution. Indeed, one of the difficulties of estimating the overall effect of marijuana legalization on the Mexican DTOs is that we do not know how involved they will be in the domestic distribution of "legal" marijuana smuggled from California. These projections require good information about the current level of involvement.

CHAPTER SIX

How Could a Reduction in Marijuana Revenues Influence Mexican Drug-Trafficking Organizations?

The previous chapters have estimated, for Mexican DTOs, both revenues now generated by U.S. drug markets and how these figures might be affected by the legalization of marijuana production in California. Although these estimates are of interest in themselves, we are ultimately most concerned about how this revenue decline will affect Mexican society. That, in turn, depends largely on how Mexican DTOs respond to a decline in revenues. To what extent will the DTOs compensate for the loss of revenues by downsizing versus shifting to other activities, and how violent would any substitute activities be? In particular, will this increase or decrease the level of violence in their operations (against competitors, the government, and citizens)?

This question takes us into a very speculative realm. There are no operationalized models of what determines the extent of violence in illegal markets, let alone models specific to Mexico. Nor is there any formal modeling of what determines the extent of specialization of criminal groups. Thus, we rely on two modes of reasoning to consider these questions. First, are there any compelling historical analogies that might provide guidance? Second, what can be learned from broad principles of organizational behavior?

The effects are likely to be specific to the conditions and nature of the organizations. Thus, we begin with a brief characterization of the DTOs themselves in their current form.

Mexican Drug-Trafficking Organizations: Activities and Capacities

Sources

There is a modest body of scholarly literature in English on the nature of Mexican DTOs. A recent project from the Mexico Institute at the Woodrow Wilson International Center for Scholars and the Trans-Border Institute at the University of San Diego has provided a good summary of many aspects of drug trafficking in Mexico (see, e.g., Shirk, 2010; Reuter, 2010).

All organized crime attracts a good deal of unverifiable claims about how much groups involved earn. This is by no means a peculiarly Mexican phenomenon. For example, the most prominent scholarly work on the American Mafia in the 1960s, by a distinguished criminologist, cited without any skepticism the claim of one leader that the organization was "bigger than General Motors" (Cressey, 1969), which was not the case (Reuter, 1983). The difficulty is that, for Mexico, there are almost no alternative sources to the press, in either Mexico or the United States, which typically reports whatever large number a government agency chooses to provide. The Mexican government publishes little; the U.S. government documents are thinly sourced; and there is minimal scholarly literature. To our knowledge, no documents reflect the kind of detailed information that can be provided by lengthy wiretaps, the "turning" of a few leading figures into informants, or the capture of the financial accounts of major organizations. In contrast, a good deal has been learned about the finances and structures of Colombian DTOs from many sources, such as the seizure of the computer of a senior Fuerzas Armadas Revolucionarias de Colombia (FARC, or Revolutionary Armed Forces of Colombia) official involved in its drug dealing.[1] Understanding the Italian Mafia was greatly helped by the lengthy statements of *pentiti*, former senior figures who turned to the government for protection against revenge by their former associates (see, e.g., Paoli, 2003). Wiretaps on the American Mafia illuminated its workings (see, e.g., Jacobs and Gouldin, 1999).

Characterizing Mexican Drug-Trafficking Organizations

Although there are independent smugglers and traffickers, the industry is thought to be dominated by a small number of large organizations; Dudley (2010) lists seven major DTOs in Mexico in 2009. These organizations appear to be hierarchical, with well-identified bosses and senior leadership, and durable, in the sense that some of them, such as the Sinaloa and Gulf cartels,[2] have survived the removal of the head of the organization. The configuration of organizations is not stable; new DTOs emerge from established ones. For example, the Zetas, now a major trafficking group, were originally a set of ex-soldiers hired by the Gulf cartel to provide enforcement services.

The older DTOs originated in the marijuana trade of the 1970s, when Mexico first established its dominance in supplying the U.S. market (Astorga and Shirk, 2010). Many of the leaders come from the state of Sinaloa, on the northern Pacific coast of the country. There is no suggestion that any of the major DTOs specializes in a particular drug. Given that the Mexican DTOs traffic in multiple substances, it is virtually impossible to identify how much of the DTO violence is attributable to the marijuana trade versus other substances.[3] Indeed, marijuana-related violence may currently be a small part of the overall violence landscape in Mexico, in which case the effects of Prop 19's passage would be potentially further diminished. However, one must also consider that marijuana may influence violence by keeping some potentially violent individuals on DTO payrolls and/or providing revenue that is used to purchase weapons and ammunition.

---

[1] See, for example, the use made of these materials in an analysis by Strasser and Barden (2010).

[2] The term *cartel* is routinely used in the popular and official literatures. They are certainly not cartels in the economic sense, as noted by Astorga and Shirk (2010). We occasionally use the term *cartel* when reporting the standard statements simply because it is familiar.

[3] If there is violence specifically related to the marijuana trade in Mexico, it involves high-level rather than retail distribution. In general, marijuana-related violence at the retail level is regarded as slight, though this claim is occasionally contested by police. There are many factors that may explain this, including (1) the relatively low value of the stock held by the individual dealers, (2) the low share of transactions involving professional dealers and the high share that involve friends and social networks, (3) the modest average levels of criminality among the buyers, and (4) the fact that buyers are able to stockpile the drug and so buy less frequently and less urgently. At the production level, there is no indication of high levels of violence for any drug. For example, farmers are not raided for their stocks of opium or coca base. It is hard to identify factors that would distinguish marijuana from other drugs at that level, in terms of incentives for violence. The violence in source countries centers around high-level distribution, and most of this research focuses on cocaine and heroin. We do not know of any research on this that is specific to high-level marijuana trafficking in Mexico. There is some research about Morocco, where hashish is an important export market. The one study of this trade that includes comments on violence (Gamella and Jimenez Rodrigo, 2008) observed low levels of violence in Spain, the first entry point for the drug into Europe, and provided no evidence on Morocco.

All the DTOs are well connected with both police and politics. The evidence of connections to the police is strong; there are numerous cases in which senior police officials have been convicted of taking money from DTOs for providing information (for example, see Stevenson, 2008). In 1997, the most senior Mexican drug official was convicted on corruption charges. The evidence for connections with politicians is less strong; very few have been convicted of taking drug money. Some analysts, such as Astorga and Shirk (2010), think it is significant that trafficking is still concentrated in states controlled by Mexico's long-time ruling party, the Partido Revolucionario Institucional (PRI, or Institutional Revolutionary Party); however, causality cannot be established.

Corruption of police for one purpose can facilitate corruption for other purposes (e.g., first drug smuggling, then kidnapping) and is important for understanding the organization of drug markets. The deep corruption of law enforcement agencies has led to the frequent reorganization of police and prosecutors. For example, after the torture and murder of DEA agent Enrique Camarena in 1985, the federal police (Dirección Federal de Seguridad, DFS or Federal Security Directorate), which had been thoroughly implicated, was disbanded and a new organization created. Many other reorganizations of policing and drug enforcement have occurred at the federal level. However, this has not prevented the emergence of major corruption cases in these reconstituted agencies. Even in August 2010, four years after President Felipe Calderón had launched his campaign against drug traffickers, authorities dismissed 10 percent of the federal police for drug-related corruption reasons in a number of agencies (Thomson, 2010).

The corruption at the level of local police has also been massive. For example, in late 2009, it was reported that 90 percent of Tijuana's police had failed federal security tests (Spagat, 2009)

Finally, we note that what we observe in 2010 is hardly a stable equilibrium. The changes in Mexican politics have had important consequences for the DTOs. Some form of tacit agreement between the PRI-run governments of Mexico and the DTOs through the 1980s and most of the 1990s enabled them to operate without a great deal of competitive conflict or incentives to threaten the government. The election of Vicente Fox of the Partido Acción Nacional (PAN, or National Action Party) disturbed that arrangement but did so without generating massive violence. The aggressive campaign of President Calderón since 2006 created an entirely new situation, resulting in rapid turnover in DTO leadership and probably disturbing existing market division arrangements (Reuter, 2010). In considering the consequences of a sudden and large decline in a major market, it is necessary to take into account the likely actions of the state, creating yet another source of uncertainty for projections.[4]

The Nondrug Activities of Drug-Trafficking Organizations

A literature search focused on media and government produced the following list of non–drug-related criminal activities in which DTOs participated: extortion, kidnapping, human trafficking, human smuggling (payment for helping an illegal immigrant cross a border[5]), and oil theft.

---

[4] A reviewer notes that, "With presidential elections looming in 2012, it is especially unclear whether another rearrangement is in store in the near future."

[5] As distinguished from human trafficking, in which the immigrant is then exploited in the destination country. The distinction is not a sharp one. Most descriptions of the Mexico border activities emphasize the smuggling rather than trafficking.

For each of these non–drug-related criminal activities, there are claims that the DTOs have become increasingly involved because of declines in their revenues from drug trafficking. Examples include the following:

- An article covering the massacre of 72 migrant workers stated that "stronger police enforcement in the Mexico drug war is pushing criminal gangs into side businesses such as extortion, kidnapping, and human trafficking" (Llana, 2010). This theme has appeared in the *Washington Post* as well: "The crackdown has led the cartels to diversify their operations, moving from the transshipment of narcotics to extortion, immigrant smuggling and kidnapping" (Booth and Fainaru, 2009).
- "[Calderón's] national housecleaning efforts have led drug gangs to hedge risks to their bread-and-butter business by going into other lucrative markets like oil products," says Strategic Forecasting's (STRATFOR's) Stephen Meiners (Bogan, 2009).
- The attorney general of Mexico, Eduardo Medina-Mora, told the Associated Press, "This is reflecting how they are melting down in terms of capabilities, how they are losing the ability to produce income. . . . To make up for lost drug profits, the gangs are morphing into powerful organized crime syndicates that are terrorizing Mexicans through kidnapping and extortion, crimes that are spreading into the U.S." ("Progress in Mexico Drug War Is Blood-Drenched," 2009).

As discussed earlier in this chapter, we do not have documented systematic estimates of the potential revenues or how these have changed over time. In assessing what the DTOs earn from non–drug-related criminal activities, there are three distinct problems:

1. estimating the number of incidents generated by a particular activity
2. estimating the average value of each incident
3. assessing what share of the business is accounted for by the DTOs.

Consider, for example, human smuggling, which occurs routinely along the U.S.–Mexican border. A 2009 *Los Angeles Times* story (Meyer, 2009) reported,

> Mexican drug cartels and their vast network of associates have branched out from their traditional business of narcotics trafficking and are now playing a central role in the multibillion-dollar-a-year business of illegal immigrant smuggling, U.S. law enforcement officials and other experts say. The business of smuggling humans across the Mexican border has always been brisk, with many thousands coming across every year.

From both the press and from scholarly studies,[6] we can establish that the price for providing passage across the border is probably about $2,500. Thus, even if the number of crossings is 100,000, which is higher than the standard figure in press stories, the total annual income would only be $250 million. No one offers any basis for determining what share of this income is accounted for by DTO involvement. As a result, it is impossible to confidently offer even an order-of-magnitude estimate of DTO human-smuggling revenues, but it is probably in the tens to low hundreds of millions of dollars.

---

[6] These studies are based on surveys of immigrants, legal and illegal, who report details of their experience in entering the United States, including what they paid for assistance; see, for example, Massey and Durand, 2003.

Are there other large potential markets into which DTOs might move in the future? One reviewer suggested that, with prescription drug prices much lower in Mexico than in the United States, the DTOs could enter the growing market for diverted prescription drugs; indeed, it is surprising that we have not already heard of this happening. This could reflect the fact that many users acquire these drugs through social networks rather than commercial markets. We are unaware of other large illegal markets, such as gambling or loan-sharking, that might provide new sources of revenues. One possibility is that DTOs organize petty crime or industrialize theft. For example, they might take over the handling of stolen cars, which has occasionally been an organized crime activity in other countries, such as Poland and Russia in the 1990s.

Another possibility is extortion, which is potentially a very large revenue source. A growing middle class and weak civil society in Mexico provide an increasingly attractive opportunity. Given the incentives for *not* reporting this crime to the police, it is impossible to estimate the scale of this activity.

Thus, we cannot provide a credible estimate of the value of DTO nondrug revenues or how this value has changed over time. Indeed, we believe that no agency of the Mexican or U.S. government can provide such an estimate. It is likely that drugs still dominate the DTO revenues, but that is merely a judgment, not a definitive statement.

Analogies

We considered analogous situations to be ones in which well-articulated criminal organizations (as opposed to networks[7]) were confronted with a loss of a market that had been a major revenue source, perhaps as the result of a change in law or change in tastes.

The most compelling analogy is to the repeal of the alcohol prohibition in the United States in 1933, which deprived the American Mafia of its principal illegal market. Although bootlegging was its most important activity, the gangs that came to constitute the Mafia were always active in other vice activities, such as gambling and prostitution (Reppetto, 2004). They had also become active in labor racketeering, using their power in corrupt unions to organize market-sharing agreements among employers, exploiting both union members and firms (Block, 1980).

Thus, despite the emphasis on bootlegging, these gangs had always been involved in multiple activities. Their principal assets were their reputation for being able to deliver on contingent threats of violence, which allowed them to serve as guarantors of agreements and as insurers within the criminal world, and their control of corrupt police departments. Schelling (1967) suggested that, in fact, it was often the police department that was using the Mafia to collect the economic rents that were available from the police department's monopoly authority in these markets.

While the repeal of prohibition surely reduced Mafia revenues, the organization continued to function in its other markets and racketeering. It might have increased its involvement in illegal gambling, another major market in the 1930s; there is a small literature arguing that Mafiosi entered into some gambling markets traditionally controlled by local gangs (Block,

---

[7] There are numerous illegal markets in which the operating entities are not hierarchical and enduring but instead consist of coalitions among offenders with complementary skills. See Bruinsma and Bernasco (2004).

1980). There was a sharp decline in the number of homicides in the United States following the repeal; plausibly, a large share of that decline was accounted for by fewer killings in the bootlegging trade. The Mafia was also active in the black markets that sprang up during World War II as a result of rationing. In a few cities, they became important in the heroin market in the 1960s. The decline of the Mafia in the 1980s, to near extinction outside of New York by 2000, represented a confluence of factors, including an innovative federal law enforcement campaign, changing migration patterns, and changes in the structure of politics in American cities (Jacobs, 1999; Reuter, 1995).

Bootlegging was probably instrumental in developing a national coalition of local criminal groups. There were specific reasons for cooperation across cities that had not existed before; for example, neither prostitution nor casino gaming required collaboration between Chicago and New York, in contrast to the illegal liquor market, with its dependence on international smuggling. The very large revenues from bootlegging enabled the gangs to be more influential in politics than they had previously been, and they developed assets that survived the loss of this market.

One difference between the American Mafia in the 1930s and the contemporary Mexican DTOs is the level of government at which they operate. Mexican DTOs have been able to corrupt major federal agencies. The American Mafia operated primarily at the state and local level, in part because, until the 1960s, the federal government had a modest role in criminal justice enforcement, notwithstanding the reputation of the Federal Bureau of Investigation (FBI) under J. Edgar Hoover (Navasky, 1971).

Do the Mexican DTOs have the same assets as the American Mafia did at the time of the repeal of Prohibition? They certainly possess reputation, i.e., the capacity to issue credible contingent threats of violence. They also have strong connections to the police throughout Mexico and to politicians in some states. In addition, they have funds and workers that allow them to be important players in elections. They might be smaller after the loss of the marijuana market but still retain their core capacities and continue to undermine the legitimacy and authority of the government. Thus, they seem very similar to the Mafia in 1933. However, in contrast to the Mafia gangs, among which violent conflict had become rare by the 1930s, the Mexican gangs have been unable to create stable working relationships, at least when under pressure from the government.

Another potential analogy is the decline of illegal gambling in the United States. It was often asserted in the period 1935 to 1975 that gambling was the principal source of revenue for the Mafia, postrepeal of Prohibition. The gambling took three general forms: numbers (a type of lottery), bookmaking (at first on horses, then on sports), and casino gaming. After 1975, an increasing share of the population had access to legal forms of gambling, with the exception of sports betting. Unfortunately, for our purposes, the Mafia was already in decline for other reasons, so it is hard to identify the specific effect of this event.

Since the Mafia's decline in the 1970s and 1980s, it has not apparently been succeeded by any other broad-based criminal organization. The Colombian drug traffickers, who may have a variety of criminal activities in their own country, do not appear to have moved beyond drug trafficking in the United States.

We are unaware of other analogous situations. Partly, this is a consequence of the absence of many other countries in which criminal gangs have become as powerful as the Mexican DTOs. Colombia is one country where DTOs did indeed become immensely powerful. However, the attacks by the Medellín and Cali gangs in the late 1980s and 1990s, and the government's effective response to those attacks, make it impossible to separately identify the consequences of the decline in drug revenues that has occurred over the past 20 years.

General Principles

We consider here the consequences of a decline in the demand for Mexican drug exports from the perspective of economic and organizational principles. There is nothing about the analysis that is specific to marijuana or to its legalization. This analysis simply assesses the effects of a loss of revenue from one of the existing streams of the DTOs resulting from some event over which they have no control, be it a change in law or in U.S. customer tastes. Our principal focus is on violence.[8]

The DTOs can be defined as consisting of the following: (1) a set of hierarchical relationships that allow higher-level members to command their subordinates to commit violent and risky actions, (2) a reputation for providing above-market earning opportunities to low-skilled workers willing to take particular kinds of risks, (3) a network of relationships with corrupt law enforcement officials, (4) a network of suppliers and customers for various drugs, and (5) ready access to capital for illegal ventures.

Presumably, the DTO demand for labor will decline, at least at the aggregate level. Given the lack of specialization, one would think almost all the individual DTOs will suffer some decline. One question is whether those "reductions in force" can be achieved through "natural attrition" or whether they will require "layoffs," to use familiar industrial jargon.

Large-scale dismissals might carry a peculiar risk, both for the organization and for society in general. Those who are fired may try to create their own organizations, so DTO managers may have to think strategically about whom to dismiss. Also, those leaving have probably become accustomed to earning levels they cannot attain in legal trade. Since the whole industry would be affected by the downturn, other DTOs will not be hiring. Thus, the fired agents might attempt to compete with their former employers.

Hence, in the short run, there could be additional violence resulting from at least three sources:

- conflict between the current leaders and the dismissed labor
- within DTOs. Even after the firing of excess labor, the earnings of the leadership most likely will decline. One way the individual manager might compensate for this is to eliminate his or her superior, generating systemic internal violence from senior managers who become more suspicious in the face of the overall decline in earnings.
- between DTOs. The leadership of an individual DTO may try to maintain their earnings by eliminating close competitors.

However, there is at least one countervailing factor that might reduce violence in the short run. Given that the signal of market decline will be strong and unambiguous, experienced participants might accept the fact that their earnings and the market as a whole are in decline. This could lead to a reduced effort on their part to fight for control of routes or officials, since

---

[8]   A reviewer notes that, to the extent that marijuana is sometimes used as an in-kind payment by the Mexican DTOs to distributors within the United States, marijuana legalization could, in effect, increase the costs of purchasing their services.

those areas of control are now less valuable. Of course, that does presume strategic thinking in a population that appears to have a propensity for expressive and instrumental violence.[9]

The natural projection in the long run is more optimistic. Fewer young males will enter the drug trade, and the incentives for violence will decline as the economic returns to leadership of a DTO fall.[10] However, the long run is indeterminably measured: probably years, and perhaps many years.

The outcome, either in the short or long term, of a substantial decline in the U.S. market for Mexican marijuana in 2011 is a matter of conjecture. One view is that, in the short run, there could be more violence as the DTO leadership faces a very disturbing change in circumstances. The fact that a decline in their share of the marijuana market would come after a period in which there has been rapid turnover at the top of their organizations and much change in their relationships with corrupt police could make it particularly difficult for the DTOs to reach a cooperative accommodation to their shrunken market. However, if the Mexican government lessens pressures and signals its willingness to reach an accommodation with a more collaborative set of DTOs, the result could be a reduction in violence.

In the long run, the analysis is different. One would think that DTO participation would become less attractive. However, the government's actions are again capable of reversing this. The government might take advantage of the weakened state of its adversary to break up the larger DTOs; a configuration of many smaller organizations could lead to greater competitive violence.

It is important to remember, though, that the estimated loss in DTO drug export revenues—even when thinking just of marijuana revenue and even if the U.S. federal government sits idly by while diverted Californian marijuana takes over the U.S. market—will be significant but not overwhelming, on the order of 13–23 percent. That is probably much smaller than the Mafia's relative loss of revenue from the repeal of Prohibition. It is also smaller than the decline in the overall drug market in the United States over the past 20 years, during which prices have declined substantially while quantities have fallen modestly. Thus, it is possible that whatever effect marijuana legalization might have on DTO violence, holding all else equal, the actual effect might not be easy to observe against a backdrop of other changes.

In summary, the effect of reducing DTO marijuana revenues on violence is a matter of conjecture. The effect on violence could well change over time.

---

[9] *Expressive violence* is force used for personal and emotional reasons. *Instrumental violence* is force for the purposes of accomplishing a functional goal. It is a common distinction in criminology.

[10] A reviewer notes that this could happen regardless of legalization, as the number of young males has steadily declined in recent generations.

CHAPTER SEVEN

Conclusion

This paper helps inform two questions that receive a considerable amount of attention within California and throughout the hemisphere: What are the potential effects of marijuana legalization? And what can the United States do to help reduce the violence in Mexico? Regardless of what happens in November with Prop 19, legalization and the security situation in Mexico will remain on the policy agenda in the United States, Mexico, and elsewhere.

Our goal was not to provide comprehensive answers to both questions, but rather to look at their intersection. Both of these issues are complex, and much of the data needed to address them do not exist or are of poor quality. This paper provides insights about how marijuana legalization in California could influence the revenues of Mexican DTOs and, hence, by extension, the related violence. There is much more work to be done, and we hope this paper stimulates others to pursue this important, policy-relevant topic.

The report yields six key findings:

- Mexican DTOs' gross revenues from moving marijuana across the border into the United States and selling it to wholesalers is likely less than $2 billion, and our preferred estimate is closer to $1.5 billion. This is far below some government and media estimates.
- The ubiquitous claim that 60 percent of Mexican DTO revenues come from U.S. marijuana consumption should not be taken seriously. Our analysis—though preliminary on this point—suggests that 15–26 percent is a more credible range for export revenues.
- California accounts for about one-seventh of U.S. marijuana consumption, and domestic production is already stronger in California than elsewhere in the United States. Hence, if Prop 19 affects only revenues from supplying marijuana to California, DTO drug export revenue losses would be very small, on the order of 2–4 percent.
- The only way Prop 19 could importantly cut DTO drug export revenues is if California-produced marijuana were smuggled to other states at prices that outcompete current Mexican supplies. If that happens, then California production could undercut sales of Mexican marijuana throughout much of the United States, cutting DTOs' marijuana export revenues by more than 65 percent and probably by 85 percent or more. In this scenario, the DTOs would lose approximately 20 percent of their total drug export revenues.
- The extent of such smuggling will depend on a number of factors, including the posture the U.S. federal government takes toward domestic cultivation and distribution. It also depends on the actions of other states, as well as the taxes and other regulations imposed on marijuana sales in California.
- Projections about whether reductions in DTO export revenues for marijuana will lead to corresponding decreases in violence are particularly uncertain; however, there are some

mechanisms that suggest that a large decline in revenues might provoke increased violence in the short run and a decline after some years.

Our estimates reflect the well-known and well-studied weaknesses of the underlying data systems on which they were built. While we are more confident of our marijuana estimates than we are for the other drugs, important limitations remain. These marijuana estimates have greater validity than most existing estimates, but, more important, they provide a documented and replicable procedure for estimating Mexican DTOs' earnings from exporting marijuana and other drugs to the United States. This stands in marked contrast to the lack of documentation and transparency in many—although of course not all—existing methods.[1]

Existing estimates about drug production and consumption are cryptic, inconsistent, and often impossible to verify. Apart from the series of studies titled *What America's Users Spend on Illegal Drugs* that was produced in the 1990s under ONDCP's auspices (see Rhodes, 1995, and Abt Associates, 2001) and the 1990s work of the Drug Availability Steering Committee (2002), many of the most-quoted estimates are not documented in a manner that allows others to assess their credibility, let alone replicate them. The large year-to-year changes in official estimates of consumption and particularly of production reduce their credibility, given the stable data on marijuana use in the U.S. population over the past decade (Table 2.1 in Chapter Two).

While a number of estimates are described as being "intelligence based" or are released by intelligence agencies, this does not mean we should automatically give them high credibility. This paper identifies a number of these estimates from national and international sources that are simply implausible. Drug-market estimation is a field plagued by a lack of data and heavily dependent on assumptions; thus, estimates from both intelligence and nonintelligence agencies need to be scrutinized. Policymakers would be well served by preventing the publication of figures without peer review. If the truth is that these figures are estimated imprecisely, that fact should be noted.

Since this report is largely focused on marijuana and generating demand-side estimates, we conclude with some brief thoughts about how to improve existing data-collection efforts to generate new information about amount consumed and expenditures. The most obvious recommendation is to start asking questions about amounts consumed per use-day (with separate questions about consumption on last use-day and consumption on a typical day) and the method of consumption (e.g., joint, bong, edible). Information about quality will also be important, and it could be the case that a simple categorical variable could prove most useful (e.g., ditchweed, commerical grade, and sinsemilla, or low, medium, and high).

Both NSDUH and ADAM made important improvements by adding questions about recent purchases' sizes and prices, and these questions should be continued. Adding choices about medical-marijuana dispensaries and collectives no longer seems frivolous, given that a growing number of states allow these modes of supply. It is paramount, however, that SAMHSA create a mechanism by which researchers can analyze NSDUH data with state and county identifiers (which is currently prohibited). This does not require open release of such data; analysis could be done in a secure facility in Rockville, Maryland, or at one of the U.S. Census Bureau's state data centers. Demand-side estimates could be dramatically improved if

---

[1]   The Drug Availability Steering Committee's (2002) work is an example of a government report that is frank about its methods and their limitations. Regrettably, it is virtually unique in this regard.

analysts were better able to assess and understand the variation in marijuana markets across subnational jurisdictions.

Bibliography

Abrams, Donald I., Hector P. Vizoso, Starley B. Shade, Cheryl Jay, Mary Ellen Kelly, and Neal L. Benowitz, "Vaporization as a Smokeless Cannabis Delivery System: A Pilot Study," *Clinical Pharmacology and Therapeutics*, Vol. 82, No. 5, November 2007, pp. 572–578.

Abt Associates, *What America's Users Spend on Illegal Drugs*, Washington, D.C.: Executive Office of the President, Office of National Drug Control Policy, December 2001. As of October 4, 2010: http://purl.access.gpo.gov/GPO/LPS20925

ADAM—*See* Arrestee Drug Abuse Monitoring Program.

Arrestee Drug Abuse Monitoring Program, *Arrestee Drug Abuse Monitoring: Annual Report*, 1987.

———, *Arrestee Drug Abuse Monitoring: Annual Report*, 1988.

———, *Arrestee Drug Abuse Monitoring: Annual Report*, 1989.

———, *Arrestee Drug Abuse Monitoring: Annual Report*, 1990.

———, *Arrestee Drug Abuse Monitoring: Annual Report*, 1991.

———, *Arrestee Drug Abuse Monitoring: Annual Report*, 1992.

———, *Arrestee Drug Abuse Monitoring: Annual Report*, 1993.

———, *Arrestee Drug Abuse Monitoring: Annual Report*, 1994.

———, *Arrestee Drug Abuse Monitoring: Annual Report*, 1995.

———, *Arrestee Drug Abuse Monitoring: Annual Report*, 1996.

———, *Arrestee Drug Abuse Monitoring: Annual Report*, 1997.

———, *Arrestee Drug Abuse Monitoring: Annual Report*, 1998. As of October 4, 2010: http://dx.doi.org/10.3886/ICPSR02826

———, *Arrestee Drug Abuse Monitoring: Annual Report*, 1999. As of October 4, 2010: http://dx.doi.org/10.3886/ICPSR02994

———, *Arrestee Drug Abuse Monitoring: Annual Report*, 2000. As of October 4, 2010: http://dx.doi.org/10.3886/ICPSR03270

———, *Arrestee Drug Abuse Monitoring: Annual Report*, 2001. As of October 4, 2010: http://dx.doi.org/10.3886/ICPSR03688

———, *Arrestee Drug Abuse Monitoring: Annual Report*, 2002. As of October 4, 2010: http://dx.doi.org/10.3886/ICPSR03815

———, *Arrestee Drug Abuse Monitoring: Annual Report*, 2003. As of October 4, 2010: http://dx.doi.org/10.3886/ICPSR04020

Astorga, Luis, and David A. Shirk, *Drug Trafficking Organizations and Counter-Drug Strategies in the U.S.-Mexican Context*, San Diego, Calif.: Evolving Democracy, Center for U.S.-Mexican Studies, University of California, San Diego, January 1, 2010. As of October 4, 2010: http://www.escholarship.org/uc/item/8j647429

Azorlosa, J. L., M. K. Greenwald, and M. L. Stitzer, "Marijuana Smoking: Effects of Varying Puff Volume and Breathhold Duration," *Journal of Pharmacology and Experimental Therapeutics*, Vol. 272, No. 2, February 1995, pp. 560–569.

Bachman, J. G., L. D. Johnston, and P. M. O'Malley, *Monitoring the Future: Questionnaire Responses from the Nation's High School Seniors*, 1976, Ann Arbor, Mich.: Institute for Social Research, 1980a.

———, *Monitoring the Future: Questionnaire Responses from the Nation's High School Seniors*, 1978, Ann Arbor, Mich.: Institute for Social Research, 1980b.

———, *Monitoring the Future: Questionnaire Responses from the Nation's High School Seniors*, 1980, Ann Arbor, Mich.: Institute for Social Research, 1981.

———, *Monitoring the Future: Questionnaire Responses from the Nation's High School Seniors*, 1982, Ann Arbor, Mich.: Institute for Social Research, 1984.

———, *Monitoring the Future: Questionnaire Responses from the Nation's High School Seniors*, 1984, Ann Arbor, Mich.: Institute for Social Research, 1985.

———, *Monitoring the Future: Questionnaire Responses from the Nation's High School Seniors*, 1986, Ann Arbor, Mich.: Institute for Social Research, 1987.

———, *Monitoring the Future: Questionnaire Responses from the Nation's High School Seniors*, 1988, Ann Arbor, Mich.: Institute for Social Research, 1991.

———, *Monitoring the Future: Questionnaire Responses from the Nation's High School Seniors*, 1990, Ann Arbor, Mich.: Institute for Social Research, 1993a.

———, *Monitoring the Future: Questionnaire Responses from the Nation's High School Seniors*, 1992, Ann Arbor, Mich.: Institute for Social Research, 1993b.

———, *Monitoring the Future: Questionnaire Responses from the Nation's High School Seniors*, 1994, Ann Arbor, Mich.: Institute for Social Research, 1997.

———, *Monitoring the Future: Questionnaire Responses from the Nation's High School Seniors*, 1996, Ann Arbor, Mich.: Institute for Social Research, 2001a. As of October 6, 2010:
http://monitoringthefuture.org/datavolumes/1996/1996dv.pdf

———, *Monitoring the Future: Questionnaire Responses from the Nation's High School Seniors*, 1998, Ann Arbor, Mich.: Institute for Social Research, 2001b. As of October 6, 2010:
http://monitoringthefuture.org/datavolumes/1998/1998dv.pdf

———, *Monitoring the Future: Questionnaire Responses from the Nation's High School Seniors*, 2000, Ann Arbor, Mich.: Institute for Social Research, 2001c. As of October 6, 2010:
http://monitoringthefuture.org/datavolumes/2000/2000dv.pdf

———, *Monitoring the Future: Questionnaire Responses from the Nation's High School Seniors*, 2002, Ann Arbor, Mich.: Institute for Social Research, 2005a. As of October 6, 2010:
http://monitoringthefuture.org/datavolumes/2002/2002dv.pdf

———, *Monitoring the Future: Questionnaire Responses from the Nation's High School Seniors*, 2004, Ann Arbor, Mich.: Institute for Social Research, 2005b. As of October 6, 2010:
http://monitoringthefuture.org/datavolumes/2004/2004dv.pdf

———, *Monitoring the Future: Questionnaire Responses from the Nation's High School Seniors*, 2006, Ann Arbor, Mich.: Institute for Social Research, 2008. As of October 6, 2010:
http://monitoringthefuture.org/datavolumes/2006/2006dv.pdf

———, *Monitoring the Future: Questionnaire Responses from the Nation's High School Seniors*, 2008, Ann Arbor, Mich.: Institute for Social Research, 2009. As of October 6, 2010:
http://monitoringthefuture.org/datavolumes/2008/2008dv.pdf

Best, Joel, *Damned Lies and Statistics: Untangling Numbers from the Media, Politicians, and Activists*, Berkeley, Calif.: University of California Press, 2001.

Block, Alan A., *East Side, West Side: Organizing Crime in New York, 1930–1950*, Cardiff: University College Cardiff Press, 1980.

Bogan, Jesse, "Mexican Drug Gangs Diversify into Oil," *Forbes*, August 11, 2009. As of October 4, 2010: http://www.forbes.com/2009/08/11/mexico-oil-theft-business-energy-drugs.html

Bond, Brittany M., and Jonathan P. Caulkins, *Potential for Legal Marijuana Sales in California to Supply Rest of U.S.*, Santa Monica, Calif.: RAND Corporation, WR-765-RC, 2010. As of October 4, 2010: http://www.rand.org/pubs/working_papers/WR765/

Booth, William, and Steve Fainaru, "In Mexico, Fears of a 'Lost Generation,'" *Washington Post*, November 3, 2009. As of October 4, 2010: http://www.washingtonpost.com/wp-dyn/content/article/2009/11/02/AR2009110203492.html

Borunda, Daniel, "El Paso 2nd Safest U.S. City: Ranking a Contrast to Violence Across Border," *El Paso Times*, November 24, 2009. As of October 4, 2010: http://www.elpasotimes.com/ci_13854721

Bouchard, Martin, "A Capture-Recapture Derived Method to Estimate Cannabis Production in Industrialized Countries," conference paper, first annual conference of the International Society for the Study of Drug Policy, Oslo, Norway, March 22–23, 2007. As of October 6, 2010: http://www.issdp.org/conferences/oslo2007/Martin_Bouchard.pdf

———, "Towards a Realistic Method to Estimate Cannabis Production in Industrialized Countries," *Contemporary Drug Problems*, Vol. 35, No. 2–3, July 2008, pp. 291–320.

Bruinsma, Gerben, and Wim Bernasco, "Criminal Groups and Transnational Illegal Markets," *Crime, Law and Social Change*, Vol. 41, 2004, pp. 79–94.

California Secretary of State, "Proposition 19: Arguments and Rebuttals," *Official Voter Information Guide*, c. 2010. As of September 15, 2010: http://www.voterguide.sos.ca.gov/propositions/19/arguments-rebuttals.htm

Caulkins, Jonathan P., and Eric L. Sevigny, "The U.S. Causes but Cannot Solve Mexico's Drug Problems," in Tony Payan and Z. Anthony Kruszewski, eds., *A War That Can't Be Won: A Journey Through the War on Drugs*, Tucson, Ariz.: University of Arizona Press, submitted August 2010.

CJCS—*See* Criminal Justice Statistics Center.

CLEAR—*See* Los Angeles County Regional Criminal Information Clearinghouse.

Connolly, Ceci, "U.S. Worker's Case Reveals How Drug Cartels Get Help from This Side of Border," *Washington Post*, September 12, 2010. As of October 4, 2010: http://www.washingtonpost.com/wp-dyn/content/article/2010/09/11/AR2010091105087.html

Cook, Philip J., *Paying the Tab: The Costs and Benefits of Alcohol Control*, Princeton, N.J.: Princeton University Press, 2007.

Corchado, Alfredo, "Drug Czar Says U.S. Use Fueling Mexico Violence," *Dallas Morning News*, February 22, 2008. As of October 4, 2010: http://www.dallasnews.com/sharedcontent/dws/dn/latestnews/stories/022208dnintdrugs.3a98bb0.html

Cornelius, Wayne A., and David A. Shirk, *Reforming the Administration of Justice in Mexico*, Notre Dame, Ind.: University of Notre Dame Press, 2007.

Cressey, Donald R., *Theft of the Nation: The Structure and Operations of Organized Crime in America*, New York: Harper and Row, 1969.

Criminal Justice Statistics Center, "Table 3A: Total Felony Arrests by Gender, Offense and Arrest Rate Statewide," *Criminal Justice Profile*, c. 2008. As of October 5, 2010: http://stats.doj.ca.gov/cjsc_stats/prof08/00/3A.htm

DASC—*See* Drug Availability Steering Committee.

Díaz-Briseño, José, *Crossing the Mississippi: How Mexican Black Tar Heroin Moved into the Eastern United States*, Woodrow Wilson International Center for Scholars, September 2010. As of October 4, 2010: http://wilsoncenter.org/news/docs/Mexican%20Black%20Tar%20Heroin-Jos%C3%A9%20Diaz%20Brise%C3%B1o.pdf

"Distance Calculator: How Far Is It?" *Infoplease*, undated website. As of October 4, 2010:
http://www.infoplease.com/atlas/calculate-distance.html

Drug Availability Steering Committee, *Drug Availability Estimates in the United States*, Washington, D.C.: Executive Office of the President of the United States, Department of Justice, December 2002. As of October 4, 2010:
http://purl.access.gpo.gov/GPO/LPS49658

Drug Enforcement Administration, Office of Intelligence, *Illegal Drug Price/Purity Report*, Washington, D.C., annual.

———, *Cannabis Yields 1992*, Washington, D.C., c. 1993.

———, *System to Retrieve Information from Drug Evidence*, annual.

Dudley, Steven S., *Drug Trafficking Organizations in Central America:* Transportistas*, Mexican Cartels and Maras*, San Diego, Calif.: Woodrow Wilson International Center for Scholars, University of California, San Diego, May 2010. As of October 4, 2010:
http://wilsoncenter.org/topics/pubs/Drug%20Trafficking%20Organizations%20in%20Central%20America.%20Dudley.pdf

Duran-Martinez, Angelica, Gayle Hazard, and Viridiana Rios, *2010 Mid-Year Report on Drug Violence in Mexico*, San Diego, Calif.: Trans-Border Institute, Joan B. Kroc School of Peace Studies, University of San Diego, August 2010.

Everingham, Susan S., C. Peter Rydell, and Jonathan P. Caulkins, "Cocaine Consumption in the United States: Estimating Past Trends and Future Scenarios," *Socio-Economic Planning Sciences*, Vol. 29, No. 4, December 1995, pp. 305–314. As of October 4, 2010:
http://www.rand.org/pubs/reprints/RP545/

Fainaru, Steve, and William Booth, "Cartels Face an Economic Battle," *Washington Post*, October 7, 2009. As of October 4, 2010:
http://www.washingtonpost.com/wp-dyn/content/article/2009/10/06/AR2009100603847.html

Federal Bureau of Investigation, *Crime in the United States*, Washington, D.C., 2010.

Felbab-Brown, Vanda, *The Violent Drug Market in Mexico and Lessons from Colombia*, Washington, D.C.: Brookings Institution, policy paper 12, March 2009. As of October 4, 2010:
http://www.brookings.edu/~/media/Files/rc/papers/2009/03_mexico_drug_market_felbabbrown/03_mexico_drug_market_felbabbrown.pdf

Fendrich, Michael, Timothy P. Johnson, Joseph S. Wislar, Amy Hubbell, and Vina Spiehler, "The Utility of Drug Testing in Epidemiological Research: Results from a General Population Survey," *Addiction*, Vol. 99, 2004, pp. 197–208.

GAO—*See* U.S. Government Accountability Office.

Gettman, Jon, "Lost Taxes and Other Costs of Marijuana Laws," *Bulletin of Cannabis Reform*, No. 4, October 2007. As of October 4, 2010:
http://www.drugscience.org/Archive/bcr4/bcr4_index.html

Gieringer, Dale, Joseph St. Laurent, and Scott Goodrich, "Cannabis Vaporizer Combines Efficient Delivery of THC with Effective Suppression of Pyrolytic Compounds," *Journal of Cannabis Therapeutics*, Vol. 4, No. 1, 2004, pp. 7–27.

Hamsher, Jane, "Video: Just Say Now Petition Delivery to Drug Czar Gil Kerlikowske," *Firedoglake*, September 16, 2010. As of October 5, 2010:
http://fdlaction.firedoglake.com/2010/09/16/video-just-say-now-petition-delivery-to-drug-czar-gil-kerlikowske/

Harrison, Lana S., Steven S. Martin, Tihomir Enev, and Deborah Harrington, *Comparing Drug Testing and Self-Report of Drug Use Among Youths and Young Adults in the General Population*, Rockville, Md.: Department of Health and Human Services, Substance Abuse and Mental Health Services Administration, Office of Applied Studies, (SMA)07-4249, 2007.

Hoffer, Lee D., *Junkie Business: The Evolution and Operation of a Heroin Dealing Network*, Belmont, Calif.: Thomson/Wadsworth, 2006.

Ingram, Matthew C., and David A. Shirk, *Judicial Reform in Mexico: Toward a New Criminal Justice System*, San Diego, Calif.: University of San Diego, Joan B. Kroc School of Peace Studies, Trans-Border Institute, May 2010.

Jacobs, James B., and Lauryn P. Gouldin, "Cosa Nostra: The Final Chapter?" *Crime and Justice*, Vol. 25, 1999, pp. 129–190.

Johnston, L. D., and J. G. Bachman, *Monitoring the Future: Questionnaire Responses from the Nation's High School Seniors, 1975*, Ann Arbor, Mich.: Institute for Social Research, 1980.

Johnston, L. D., J. G. Bachman, and P. M. O'Malley, *Monitoring the Future: Questionnaire Responses from the Nation's High School Seniors, 1977*, Ann Arbor, Mich.: Institute for Social Research, 1980a.

———, *Monitoring the Future: Questionnaire Responses from the Nation's High School Seniors, 1979*, Ann Arbor, Mich.: Institute for Social Research, 1980b.

———, *Monitoring the Future: Questionnaire Responses from the Nation's High School Seniors, 1981*, Ann Arbor, Mich.: Institute for Social Research, 1982.

———, *Monitoring the Future: Questionnaire Responses from the Nation's High School Seniors, 1983*, Ann Arbor, Mich.: Institute for Social Research, 1984.

———, *Monitoring the Future: Questionnaire Responses from the Nation's High School Seniors, 1985*, Ann Arbor, Mich.: Institute for Social Research, 1986.

———, *Monitoring the Future: Questionnaire Responses from the Nation's High School Seniors, 1987*, Ann Arbor, Mich.: Institute for Social Research, 1991.

———, *Monitoring the Future: Questionnaire Responses from the Nation's High School Seniors, 1989*, Ann Arbor, Mich.: Institute for Social Research, 1992.

———, *Monitoring the Future: Questionnaire Responses from the Nation's High School Seniors, 1991*, Ann Arbor, Mich.: Institute for Social Research, 1993.

———, *Monitoring the Future: Questionnaire Responses from the Nation's High School Seniors, 1993*, Ann Arbor, Mich.: Institute for Social Research, 1995.

———, *Monitoring the Future: Questionnaire Responses from the Nation's High School Seniors, 1995*, Ann Arbor, Mich.: Institute for Social Research, 1997.

———, *Monitoring the Future: Questionnaire Responses from the Nation's High School Seniors, 1997*, Ann Arbor, Mich.: Institute for Social Research, 2001a. As of October 6, 2010:
http://monitoringthefuture.org/datavolumes/1997/1997dv.pdf

———, *Monitoring the Future: Questionnaire Responses from the Nation's High School Seniors, 1999*, Ann Arbor, Mich.: Institute for Social Research, 2001b. As of October 6, 2010:
http://monitoringthefuture.org/datavolumes/1999/1999dv.pdf

———, *Monitoring the Future: Questionnaire Responses from the Nation's High School Seniors, 2001*, Ann Arbor, Mich.: Institute for Social Research, 2003. As of October 6, 2010:
http://monitoringthefuture.org/datavolumes/2001/2001dv.pdf

———, *Monitoring the Future: Questionnaire Responses from the Nation's High School Seniors, 2003*, Ann Arbor, Mich.: Institute for Social Research, 2005. As of October 6, 2010:
http://monitoringthefuture.org/datavolumes/2003/2003dv.pdf

———, *Monitoring the Future: Questionnaire Responses from the Nation's High School Seniors, 2005*, Ann Arbor, Mich.: Institute for Social Research, 2006. As of October 6, 2010:
http://monitoringthefuture.org/datavolumes/2005/2005dv.pdf

———, *Monitoring the Future: Questionnaire Responses from the Nation's High School Seniors, 2007*, Ann Arbor, Mich.: Institute for Social Research, 2009. As of October 6, 2010:
http://monitoringthefuture.org/datavolumes/2007/2007dv.pdf

———, *Monitoring the Future: Questionnaire Responses from the Nation's High School Seniors, 2009*, Ann Arbor, Mich.: Institute for Social Research, 2010. As of October 6, 2010:
http://monitoringthefuture.org/datavolumes/2009/2009dv.pdf

Kilmer, Beau, Jonathan P. Caulkins, Rosalie Liccardo Pacula, Robert J. MacCoun, and Peter H. Reuter, *Altered State? Assessing How Marijuana Legalization in California Could Influence Marijuana Consumption and Public Budgets*, Santa Monica, Calif.: RAND Corporation, OP-315-RC, 2010. As of October 4, 2010: http://www.rand.org/pubs/occasional_papers/OP315/

Kilmer, Beau, and Rosalie Liccardo Pacula, *Estimating the Size of the Global Drug Market: A Demand-Side Approach—Report 2*, Santa Monica, Calif.: RAND Corporation, TR-711-EC, 2009. As of October 4, 2010: http://www.rand.org/pubs/technical_reports/TR711/

Kilmer, Beau, and Peter Reuter, "Prime Numbers: Doped—The Disaster Drugs: Heroin and Cocaine," *Foreign Policy*, November–December 2009. As of October 4, 2010: http://www.foreignpolicy.com/articles/2009/10/19/prime_numbers_doped

Kleiman, Mark, *When Brute Force Fails: How to Have Less Crime and Less Punishment*, Princeton, N.J.: Princeton University Press, 2009.

Leggett, T., "A Review of the World Cannabis Situation," *Bulletin on Narcotics*, Vol. LVIII, No. 1–2, 2006, pp. 1–3.

Levitt, Steven D., Sudhir Alladi Venkatesh, "An Economic Analysis of a Drug-Selling Gang's Finances," *Quarterly Journal of Economics*, Vol. 115, No. 3, August 2000, pp. 755–789.

Llana, Sara Miller, "Mexico Massacre: How the Drug War Is Pushing Cartels into Human Trafficking," *Christian Science Monitor*, August 30, 2010. As of October 4, 2010: http://www.csmonitor.com/World/Americas/2010/0830/Mexico-massacre-How-the-drug-war-is-pushing-cartels-into-human-trafficking

Los Angeles County Regional Criminal Information Clearinghouse, "2nd Quarter 2007 Drug Price List," c. 2007. As of October 4, 2010: https://www.laclear.com/Secure/Publications/2nd%20Qtr%20Tri-fold%20drug%20price%20list.pdf

"Marijuana Prices in the U.S.A.," *Narcotic News*, web page, undated. As of February 7, 2010: http://www.narcoticnews.com/marijuana-prices-in-the-U.S.A.php

Massey, Douglas S., and Jorge Durand, "The Costs of Contradiction: U.S. Immigration Policy 1986–1996," *Latino Studies*, Vol. 1, No. 2, 2003, pp. 233–252.

Medina-Mora, María Elena, Guilherme Borges, Clara Fleiz, Corina Benjet, Estela Rojas, Joaquín Zambrano, Jorge Villatoro, and Sergio Aguilar-Gaxiola, "Prevalence and Correlates of Drug Use Disorders in Mexico," *Revista Panamericana de Salud Pública*, Vol. 19, No. 4, April 2006, pp. 265–276.

Meyer, Josh, "Drug Cartels Raise the Stakes on Human Smuggling," *Los Angeles Times*, March 23, 2009. As of October 4, 2010: http://articles.latimes.com/2009/mar/23/nation/na-human-smuggling23

Monitoring the Future, "Teen Marijuana Use Tilts Up, While Some Drugs Decline in Use," press release, Ann Arbor, Mich., December 14, 2009. As of October 6, 2010: http://monitoringthefuture.org/pressreleases/09drugpr.pdf

Narcotic News, website. As of October 5, 2010: http://www.narcoticnews.com/

Natarajan, Mangai, and M. Belanger, "Varieties of Upper-level Drug Dealing Organizations: A Typology of Cases Prosecuted in New York City," *Journal of Drug Issues*, Vol. 28, No. 4, 1998, pp. 1005–1026.

National Drug Intelligence Center, "Drug Market Analyses," undated web page. As of October 4, 2010: http://www.justice.gov/ndic/topics/dmas.htm

———, *California Northern and Eastern Districts Drug Threat Assessment*, Johnstown, Pa.: U.S. Department of Justice, National Drug Intelligence Center, January 2001a. As of October 6, 2010: http://purl.access.gpo.gov/GPO/LPS36404

———, *California Central District Drug Threat Assessment*, Johnstown, Pa.: U.S. Department of Justice, National Drug Intelligence Center, May 2001b. As of October 4, 2010: http://purl.access.gpo.gov/GPO/LPS36403

———, "Marijuana," *Wyoming Drug Threat Assessment*, December 2001c. As of October 4, 2010:
http://www.justice.gov/ndic/pubs07/712/marijuan.htm

———, *California Central District Drug Threat Assessment Update*, Johnstown, Pa.: U.S. Department of Justice, National Drug Intelligence Center, May 2002a. As of October 6, 2010:
http://www.justice.gov/ndic/pubs1/1113/index.htm

———, *Crystal Methamphetamine*, Johnstown, Pa.: U.S. Department of Justice, National Drug Intelligence Center, August 2002b. As of October 6, 2010:
http://purl.access.gpo.gov/GPO/LPS83543

———, *National Drug Threat Assessment 2004*, Johnstown, Pa.: U.S. Department of Justice, National Drug Intelligence Center, April 2004. As of October 4, 2010:
http://www.justice.gov/ndic/pubs8/8731/index.htm

———, *National Drug Threat Assessment 2005*, Johnstown, Pa.: U.S. Department of Justice, National Drug Intelligence Center, February 2005. As of October 4, 2010:
http://www.justice.gov/ndic/pubs11/12620/index.htm

———, *Arizona High Intensity Drug Trafficking Area Drug Market Analysis*, Johnstown, Pa.: National Drug Intelligence Center, U.S. Department of Justice, May 2007a. As of October 6, 2010:
http://www.justice.gov/ndic/pubs22/22934/index.htm

———, *Appalachia High Intensity Drug Trafficking Area Drug Market Analysis*, Johnstown, Pa.: National Drug Intelligence Center, U.S. Department of Justice, May 2007b. As of October 6, 2010:
http://www.justice.gov/ndic/pubs23/23935/index.htm

———, *Houston High Intensity Drug Trafficking Area Drug Market Analysis*, Johnstown, Pa.: U.S. Department of Justice, National Drug Intelligence Center, June 2007c. As of October 6, 2010:
http://www.justice.gov/ndic/pubs23/23932/index.htm

———, *National Drug Threat Assessment 2008*, Johnstown, Pa.: U.S. Department of Justice, National Drug Intelligence Center, October 2007d. As of October 6, 2010:
http://www.justice.gov/ndic/pubs25/25921/index.htm

———, *California Border Alliance Group Drug Market Analysis 2008*, Johnstown, Pa.: U.S. Department of Justice, National Drug Intelligence Center, May 2008a. As of October 6, 2010:
http://www.justice.gov/ndic/pubs27/27487/index.htm

———, *Houston High Intensity Drug Trafficking Area Drug Market Analysis 2008*, Johnstown, Pa.: U.S. Department of Justice, National Drug Intelligence Center, June 2008b. As of October 6, 2010:
http://www.justice.gov/ndic/pubs27/27493/index.htm

———, *Los Angeles High Intensity Drug Trafficking Area Drug Market Analysis 2008*, June 2008c. As of October 6, 2010:
http://www.justice.gov/ndic/pubs27/27495/index.htm

———, *National Drug Threat Assessment 2009*, Johnstown, Pa.: U.S. Department of Justice, National Drug Intelligence Center, December 2008d. As of October 4, 2010:
http://www.justice.gov/ndic/pubs31/31379/index.htm

———, *National Methamphetamine Threat Assessment 2009*, December 2008e. As of October 6, 2010:
http://www.justice.gov/ndic/pubs32/32166/index.htm

———, *National Drug Threat Assessment 2010*, Johnstown, Pa.: U.S. Department of Justice, National Drug Intelligence Center, February 2010. As of October 4, 2010:
http://www.justice.gov/ndic/pubs38/38661/index.htm

Navasky, Victor S., *Kennedy Justice*, New York: Atheneum, 1971.

NDIC—*See* National Drug Intelligence Center.

Nicosia, Nancy, Rosalie Licardo Pacula, Beau Kilmer, Russell Lundberg, and James Chiesa, *The Economic Cost of Methamphetamine Use in the United States, 2005*, Santa Monica, Calif.: RAND Corporation, MG-829-MPF/NIDA, 2009. As of October 6, 2010:
http://www.rand.org/pubs/monographs/MG829/

Office of National Drug Control Policy, *National Drug Control Strategy*, Washington, D.C., February 2006. As of October 4, 2010:
http://ncjrs.gov/App/Publications/abstract.aspx?ID=234430

———, *ADAM II: 2008 Annual Report*, Washington, D.C., 2009. As of October 4, 2010:
http://www.whitehousedrugpolicy.gov/publications/pdf/adam2008.pdf

———, *National Drug Control Strategy*, Washington, D.C., 2010a. As of October 4, 2010:
http://www.whitehousedrugpolicy.gov/publications/policy/ndcs10/index.html

———, "Statement on Mexican Drug Trafficking Organization Profits from Marijuana," September 16, 2010b. As of October 4, 2010:
http://www.whitehousedrugpolicy.gov/news/press10/MJrevenue.pdf

ONDCP—*See* Office of National Drug Control Policy.

Paoli, Letizia, *Mafia Brotherhoods: Organized Crime, Italian Style*, Oxford: Oxford University Press, 2003.

Paoli, Letizia, Victoria A. Greenfield, and Peter Reuter, *The World Heroin Market: Can Supply Be Cut?* Oxford: Oxford University Press, 2009.

"Progress in Mexico Drug War Is Blood-Drenched," Associated Press, March 10, 2009.

Pudney, Stephen, Celia Badillo, Mark Bryan, Jon Burton, Gabriella Conti, and Maria Iacovou, "Estimating the Size of the UK Illicit Drug Market," in Nicola Singleton, Rosemary Murray, and Louise Tinsley, eds., *Measuring Different Aspects of Problem Drug Use: Methodological Developments*, 2nd ed., London: Home Office, online report 16/06, 2006, pp. 46–120. As of October 4, 2010:
http://www.homeoffice.gov.uk/rds/pdfs06/rdsolr1606.pdf

Quinones, Sam, "A Lethal Business Model Targets Middle America," *Los Angeles Times*, February 14, 2010a. As of October 4, 2010:
http://articles.latimes.com/2010/feb/14/local/la-me-blacktar14-2010feb14

———, "Black Tar Moves In, and Death Follows," *Los Angeles Times*, February 15, 2010b. As of October 4, 2010:
http://articles.latimes.com/2010/feb/15/local/la-me-blacktar15-2010feb15

———, "The Good Life in Xalisco Can Mean Death in the United States," *Los Angeles Times*, February 16, 2010c. As of October 4, 2010:
http://articles.latimes.com/2010/feb/16/local/la-me-blacktar16-2010feb16

Reppetto, Thomas A., *American Mafia: A History of Its Rise to Power*, New York: Henry Holt, 2004.

Reuter, Peter H., *Disorganized Crime: The Economics of the Visible Hand*, Cambridge, Mass.: MIT Press, 1983.

———, "The (Continued) Vitality of Mythical Numbers," *Public Interest*, Vol. 75, Spring 1984, pp. 135–147. As of October 4, 2010:
http://www.nationalaffairs.com/public_interest/detail/the-continued-vitality-of-mythical-numbers

———, "The Decline of the American Mafia," *Public Interest*, Vol. 120, Summer 1995, pp. 89–99. As of October 4, 2010:
http://www.nationalaffairs.com/public_interest/detail/the-decline-of-the-american-mafia

———, "The Mismeasurement of Illegal Drug Markets: The Implications of Its Irrelevance," in Susan Pozo, ed., *Exploring the Underground Economy: Studies of Illegal and Unreported Activity*, Kalamazoo, Mich.: W. E. Upjohn Institute for Employment Research, 1996, pp. 63–80. As of October 4, 2010:
http://www.rand.org/pubs/reprints/RP613/

———, "Systemic Violence in Drug Markets," *Crime, Law and Social Change*, Vol. 52, No. 3, 2009, pp. 275–289.

———, *How Can Domestic U.S. Drug Policy Help Mexico?* San Diego, Calif.: Woodrow Wilson International Center for Scholars, July 2010. As of October 4, 2010:
http://wilsoncenter.org/news/docs/Reuter%20-%20Final.pdf

Reuter, Peter H., and Victoria A. Greenfield, "Measuring Global Drug Markets: How Good Are the Numbers and Why Should We Care About Them?" *World Economics*, Vol. 2, No. 4, October–December 2001, pp. 159–173. As of October 4, 2010:
http://www.rand.org/pubs/reprints/RP999/

Reuter, Peter, and Mark A. R. Kleiman, "Risks and Prices: An Economic Analysis of Drug Enforcement," *Crime and Justice*, Vol. 7, 1986, pp. 289–340.

Rhodes, William, *What America's Users Spend on Illegal Drugs, 1988–1993*, Washington, D.C.: Office of National Drug Control Policy, Spring 1995.

Rhodes, William, Stacia Langenbahn, Ryan Kling, and Paul Scheiman, *What America's Users Spend on Illegal Drugs, 1988–1995*, Washington, D.C.: Executive Office of the President, Office of National Drug Control Policy, September 29, 1997. As of October 6, 2010:
http://purl.access.gpo.gov/GPO/LPS53101

Rios, Viridiana, "Evaluating the Economic Impact of Drug Traffic in Mexico," unpublished working paper, c. 2010. As of September 15, 2010:
http://www-old.gov.harvard.edu/student/rios/MexicanDrugMarket_Riosv2.doc

Rosenberg, Mica, "Former Mexico President Supports Legalizing Drugs," Reuters, August 10, 2010. As of October 4, 2010:
http://www.reuters.com/article/idUSTRE6784R120100810

Sabet, Kevin, and Viridiana Rios, "Why Violence Has Increased in Mexico and What Can We Do About It?" unpublished working paper, November 28, 2009. As of October 4, 2010:
http://www.gov.harvard.edu/files/SabetRios09_VersionPostedOnline.pdf

SAMHSA—*See* Substance Abuse and Mental Health Services Administration.

Schaefer, Agnes Gereben, Benjamin Bahney, and K. Jack Riley, *Security in Mexico: Implications for U.S. Policy Options*, Santa Monica, Calif.: RAND Corporation, MG-876-RC, 2009. As of October 4, 2010:
http://www.rand.org/pubs/monographs/MG876/

Schelling, Thomas C., "Economic Analysis of Organized Crime," in Task Force on Organized Crime, *Task Force Report: Organized Crime—Annotations and Consultants' Papers*, Washington, D.C.: Government Printing Office, 1967.

Seper, Jerry, and Matthew Cella, "Signs in Arizona Warn of Smuggler Dangers," *Washington Times*, August 31, 2010. As of October 4, 2010:
http://www.washingtontimes.com/news/2010/aug/31/signs-in-arizona-warn-of-smuggler-dangers/

Shirk, David A., *Drug Violence in Mexico: Data and Analysis from 2001–2009*, San Diego, Calif.: University of San Diego, Joan B. Kroc School of Peace Studies, Trans-Border Institute, Justice in Mexico Project, January 2010. As of October 4 2010:
http://www.wilsoncenter.org/topics/pubs/2010-Shirk-JMP-Drug_Violence.pdf

Singer, Max, "The Vitality of Mythical Numbers," *Public Interest*, Vol. 23, Spring 1971. As of October 4, 2010:
http://www.nationalaffairs.com/public_interest/detail/the-vitality-of-mythical-numbers

Sistema Nacional de Seguridad Pública and Consejo Nacional de Población, "Homicidios Dolosos: Total y por Cada 100 Mil Habitantes—Registro ante Agencias del Ministerio Público de las Entidades Federativas," c. 2010. As of September 15, 2010:
http://www.icesi.org.mx/documentos/estadisticas/estadisticasOfi/denuncias_homicidio_doloso_1997_2009.pdf

Spagat, Elliot, "Mexico's Drug War Focuses on Police Corruption in Tijuana," *San Diego News Network*, December 20, 2009. As of October 4, 2010:
http://www.sdnn.com/sandiego/2009-12-20/mexico/mexicos-drug-war-focuses-on-police-corruption-in-tijuana

Stevenson, M., "Mexico's Top Federal Police Quits Amidst Probe," *Washington Post*, November 1, 2008.

Strasser, Fred, and Andrew Barden, eds., "FARC's Cocaine Sales to Mexico Cartels Prove Too Rich to Subdue," *Bloomberg Businessweek*, January 20, 2010. As of October 4, 2010:
http://www.businessweek.com/news/2010-01-20/
farc-s-cocaine-sales-to-mexico-cartels-prove-too-rich-to-subdue.html

Substance Abuse and Mental Health Services Administration, *Treatment Episode Data Set: Admissions (TEDS-A Series)*, Rockville, Md.: U.S. Department of Health and Human Services, Substance Abuse and Mental Health Services Administration, 1992–2009. As of October 4, 2010:
http://www.icpsr.umich.edu/icpsrweb/SAMHDA/series/00056

———, *Results from the 2001 National Household Survey on Drug Abuse*, Rockville, Md.: Department of Health and Human Services, Substance Abuse and Mental Health Services Administration, Office of Applied Studies, 2001. As of October 6, 2010:
http://purl.access.gpo.gov/GPO/LPS77495

———, "Instrumentation Protocol Changes," in Substance Abuse and Mental Health Services Administration, *Methodological Resource Book*, c. 2002a. As of September 15, 2010:
http://www.oas.samhsa.gov/nhsda/2k2MRB/2k2instrProChgs.pdf

———, *Results from the National Survey on Drug Use and Health (NSDUH)*, Rockville, Md.: U.S. Department of Health and Human Services, Substance Abuse and Mental Health Services Administration, 2002b.

———, *Results from the National Survey on Drug Use and Health (NSDUH)*, Rockville, Md.: U.S. Department of Health and Human Services, Substance Abuse and Mental Health Services Administration, 2003.

———, *Results from the National Survey on Drug Use and Health (NSDUH)*, Rockville, Md.: U.S. Department of Health and Human Services, Substance Abuse and Mental Health Services Administration, 2004.

———, *Results from the National Survey on Drug Use and Health (NSDUH)*, Rockville, Md.: U.S. Department of Health and Human Services, Substance Abuse and Mental Health Services Administration, 2005.

———, *Results from the National Survey on Drug Use and Health (NSDUH)*, Rockville, Md.: U.S. Department of Health and Human Services, Substance Abuse and Mental Health Services Administration, 2006.

———, "Appendix B: Tables of Model-Based Estimates (50 States and the District of Columbia), by Measure," c. 2007a. As of September 15, 2010:
http://oas.samhsa.gov/2k7state/AppB.htm

———, *Results from the National Survey on Drug Use and Health (NSDUH)*, Rockville, Md.: U.S. Department of Health and Human Services, Substance Abuse and Mental Health Services Administration, 2007b.

———, *Results from the National Survey on Drug Use and Health (NSDUH)*, Rockville, Md.: U.S. Department of Health and Human Services, Substance Abuse and Mental Health Services Administration, 2008.

TEDS—*See* SAMHSA, 1992–2009.

"Thinking the Unthinkable: Amid Drug-War Weariness, Felipe Calderón Calls for a Debate on Legalisation," *Economist*, August 12, 2010. As of October 6, 2010:
http://www.economist.com/node/16791730

Thomson, Adam, "Mexico Dismisses 10% of Federal Police," *Financial Times*, August 31, 2010. As of October 4, 2010:
http://www.ft.com/cms/s/0/6d6353a0-b491-11df-8208-00144feabdc0.html

Toonen, Marcel, Simon Ribot, and Jac Thissen, "Yield of Illicit Indoor Cannabis Cultivation in the Netherlands," *Journal of Forensic Science*, Vol. 51, No. 5, September 2006, pp. 1050–1054.

Trans-High Market Quotations, *High Times*, monthly.

United Nations Office on Drugs and Crime, Office for Drug Control and Crime Prevention, International Drug Control Programme, *World Drug Report*, c. 2006. As of October 2010:
http://www.unodc.org/unodc/en/data-and-analysis/WDR-2006.html

————, *World Drug Report*, c. 2008. As of October 4, 2010:
http://www.unodc.org/unodc/en/data-and-analysis/WDR-2008.html

————, *World Drug Report*, c. 2009. As of October 4, 2010:
http://www.unodc.org/unodc/en/data-and-analysis/WDR-2009.html

————, *World Drug Report*, c. 2010. As of October 4, 2010:
http://www.unodc.org/unodc/en/data-and-analysis/WDR-2010.html

UNODC.—*See* United Nations Office on Drugs and Crime.

U.S. Department of State, Bureau of International Narcotics Matters, Bureau of International Narcotics and Law Enforcement Affairs, *International Narcotics Control Strategy Report (INCSR)*, Washington, D.C., 1990.

————, *International Narcotics Control Strategy Report (INCSR)*, Washington, D.C., 1994.

————, *International Narcotics Control Strategy Report (INCSR)*, Washington, D.C., 2008. As of October 4, 2010:
http://www.state.gov/p/inl/rls/nrcrpt/2008/index.htm

————, *International Narcotics Control Strategy Report (INCSR)*, Washington, D.C., 2009. As of October 4, 2010:
http://www.state.gov/p/inl/rls/nrcrpt/2009/index.htm

U.S. Government Accountability Office, *Drug Control: U.S. Assistance Has Helped Mexican Counternarcotics Efforts, but Tons of Illicit Drugs Continue to Flow into the United States—Report to Congressional Requesters*, Washington, D.C., GAO-07-1018, 2007. As of October 4, 2010:
http://purl.access.gpo.gov/GPO/LPS86667

"Wholesale Marijuana Prices," *Narcotic News*, undated web page. As of October 6, 2010:
http://www.narcoticnews.com/Marijuana-Prices-in-the-U.S.A.php

Woodrow Wilson International Center for Scholars, Mexico Institute, "U.S.-Mexico Security Cooperation Portal," undated website. As of September 14, 2010:
http://www.wilsoncenter.org/index.cfm?topic_id=5949&fuseaction=topics.item&news_id=407349

Yes on 19, "About Proposition 19," *Yes on Prop 19: Control and Tax Cannabis November 2, 2010*, undated web page. As of October 4, 2010:
http://yeson19.com/about